WHOLE LANGUAGE FOR ADULTS

A GUIDE TO Instruction

Judy Cheatham

Mallory Clarke

Denise McKay

Melody Schneider

Mary Dunn Siedow

NEW READERS PRESS

Acknowledgement

Jane MacKillop was the adviser for this book, instrumental in shaping its concept, organization, and content. She also is the author of the other *Whole Language for Adults* books: *A Guide to Portfolio Assessment, A Guide to Initial Assessment,* and *A Guide to Administration and Staff Development.*

Jane has an extensive background in adult literacy and ESL. She coauthored *Improve Your English through Television* (1986) for BBC/ALBSU and coedited with Michael Holzman *The Gateway: Paths to Adult Learning* (1990), published by the Philip Morris Companies and The Mayor's Commission on Literacy in Philadelphia. She has administered programs for Literacy Volunteers of New York City, City University of New York, and Southern Westchester Board of Cooperative Education Services. Currently, she is Director of Special Programs, Office of Academic Affairs, City University of New York. _____

ISBN 1-56420-071-X

EACH ONE TEACH ONE

Copyright © 1994
New Readers Press
Publishing Division of Laubach Literacy International
Box 131, Syracuse, New York 13210-0131

9 8 7 6 5 4 3 2 1

TABLE OF CONTENTS

About the Authors

Judy Cheatham, Ph.D., is the Campbell Professor of Writing at Greensboro College, North Carolina, and director of the parenting literacy component of Guilford County Even Start Family Literacy Program. She is the national writing consultant for Literacy Volunteers of America, author of *Small Group Tutoring: Basic Reading, a Collaborative Approach for Literacy Instruction,* and coauthor of the seventh edition of *Tutor,* LVA's training manual. Active in family and workplace literacy, she has conducted adult literacy projects funded by the National Endowment for the Humanities, the U.S. Department of Education, the Kentucky Humanities Council, and the Kentucky Literacy Commission. A teacher since 1973, she lives in Greensboro with her husband, George, and children, Dayton and Sarah Hampton. _____

Mallory Clarke has an M.A. in Educational Psychology and is a certified reading teacher. Since 1974, she has taught reading, writing, math, and ESL for small groups, for large classes, and one-to-one. She has trained hundreds of tutors and teachers in student-centered, theme-based, and whole language approaches. Currently, she teaches at Seattle Central Community College. She is the author of *Discovery and Respect: A Handbook for Student-directed Group Learning,* published by Goodwill Literacy, Seattle, Washington, and is coauthor of *Dimensions of Change: An Authentic Assessment Guidebook,* available from the ABLE Network, Seattle. In May 1993, she and her husband, Pat, became parents of a daughter, Riley. _____

Denise McKay went to work at the Madison Literacy Council in 1985 when she graduated from the University of Wisconsin with B.A.'s in linguistics and French. As director of education, she is responsible for tutor training and curriculum development for both reading and ESL. She has given presentations at two Laubach Literacy national conferences on her practical techniques for teaching phonics that place skills instruction within a learner-centered, whole language approach. To expand on the phonics and word-analysis activities presented in this book, she is writing a phonics program to be published by New Readers Press. _____

Melody Schneider has a B.F.A. in acting and has worked in adult basic education since 1985 as a program manager, teacher trainer, and teacher in community-based organizations, job training programs, and a county jail. Currently she teaches at Seattle Central Community College and is a trainer developer for the state of Washington. She is coauthor of *Dimensions of Change: An Authentic Assessment Guidebook,* available from the ABLE Network, Seattle. She has developed approaches to teaching that encourage student self-expression through writing, drawing, and acting. She is an advocate of learner-centered education. A teacher trainer in instruction and assessment, she has led workshops in the United States and Canada, and written for educational publications. _____

Mary Dunn Siedow, Ed.D., is executive director of the Durham County Literacy Council in North Carolina. A teacher, reading specialist, and teacher educator, she chairs the International Reading Association's Adult Literacy Committee. She has made numerous presentations on adult literacy at national conferences and has written about literacy instruction and content-area reading, most recently for the Yearbook of the College Reading Association and the *Journal of Reading Education.* She was a contributing author for *Teaching Adult Beginning Readers: To Reach Them My Hand,* published by the College Reading Association. Mary and her husband, Jim, have lived in Durham since 1976. _____

INTRODUCTION

This book is a resource for teachers to help English-speaking adults improve their reading and writing skills. You will find it useful whether you teach ABE or GED classes, tutor new readers, or teach workplace or family literacy. Whatever your setting or program, whether you have a set curriculum and assigned core text or design your own curriculum and choose all your own materials, this book is a good resource for you. It offers you a framework for planning instruction as well as ideas, techniques, and activities to stimulate your thinking as you create meaningful and personal instruction for your students.

As teachers of adults, we share a single goal: to teach in a way that keeps students interested in learning. To do so we help students experience reading and writing as personally relevant from the first day of instruction. We provide an environment and activities that help students experience what reading and writing are: extensions of language for communicating, problem solving, learning, and having fun.

Effective teaching reflects the goals of instruction. If one goal is to stimulate and expand adult learners' abilities to read and write, then we will help students think about and relate to the ideas and words they are reading and writing. If another goal is to help students gain self-esteem and an equal footing in the larger community of readers and writers, then we will involve students as valued partners in a community of learners whose goals and ideas are heard and respected. This active, experiential approach to teaching reading and writing has deep roots in educational theory and practice.

Defining Whole Language

Teaching reading and writing as purposeful communication is often called a whole language approach. There is no single approved method, curriculum, or set of materials that is officially "whole language." Instead, whole language is an array of concepts about teaching and learning that are guides for practice.

Whole language principles help personalize instruction, bring you and your students into the center of instruction, and help you build your confidence as a teacher and your students' confidence as learners.

Key points to keep in mind:

- **Provide activities that involve reading, writing, speaking, and listening.** Written and spoken language are interrelated; each reinforces the other. The more students read, write, talk, and listen, the better readers they will become. Invite students to write, talk, and read in each session. Speaking and listening support reading and writing, and reading and writing support speaking.

- **Include writing from the beginning.** Have students begin to write from the start of reading instruction. They can use invented spelling or even drawing to communicate their ideas. From the beginning, you can fit writing into many aspects of instruction. Students can write to respond to reading, to evaluate learning and teaching, and to keep records. Students also need to learn how to write for others and develop ideas by using the writing process, which includes planning, drafting, revising, and editing. Writing as a matter of course helps students perceive themselves as writers and identify with the authors of the material they read, so that reading becomes an act of communication.

- **Provide a variety of activities and materials that are meaningful to students.** We don't read to become better at reading; we read for enjoyment and information. "Real" reading and writing occur when what we do is interesting and meaningful in itself. Reading and writing different types of material for a variety of purposes helps students expand their sense of reading and writing. It also stirs their desire to read and write. Include everyday materials, such as newspapers, magazines, and job forms, as well as textbooks, poems, and other literature.

- **Personalize instruction.** Learning happens as we connect new information with what we already know. Students bring their own life and language experiences to instruction and achieve the most when they make personal connections to what they are doing. Students can connect to instruction when you encourage them to develop and state their goals, find materials that appeal to them, and ask for their opinions.

- **Teach reading and writing skills and strategies.** Reading and writing are extremely complex acts. We aren't able to fully explain what we do when we read and write. So much about reading and writing has to be learned holistically, by actually reading and writing, and by observing experienced readers and writers in action.

  Within this approach, teaching specific aspects of reading and writing is important. Directed instruction in a particular skill is especially helpful for adults who might have to unlearn incorrect ways as well as learn new ways. Skill instruction clarifies specific points, allows for practice and mastery of a skill, and makes learning more manageable.

  A Guide to Instruction shows two ways to teach skills: in mini-lessons (a discrete activity in the middle of a session), and in "teachable moments" (times during reading and writing when students can benefit from informal help you provide). By setting aside specific activities for skill instruction and using teachable moments to help when needed, you place skill instruction in its proper perspective—as an important part of teaching and learning but not the main event.

Describing This Book

A Guide to Instruction is one in a set of four books. It is a companion book to *A Guide to Portfolio Assessment,* which gives guidance and examples for conducting performance assessment over the course of instruction.

The other two books are *A Guide to Initial Assessment,* for program personnel who do initial assessment and placement, and *A Guide to Administration and Staff Development,* for program managers and staff developers.

A Guide to Instruction is written for teachers of adult learners with a range of reading levels: new readers (readability 1–3), developing readers (readability 4–5), intermediate readers (readability 6–7, pre-GED), and advanced readers (readability 8–12, GED). It presents key instructional concepts, basic techniques, and activities. A general activity is often followed by one or more sample activities that depict specific instructional situations. Many activities take place in group or class settings, but some are for a teacher and student working one-to-one. As presented, the situations may involve students whose reading and writing skills differ from the students you are teaching. Most activities are easily adaptable for teaching students at various levels in a variety of settings.

A Guide to Instruction begins with key factors to consider when planning and designing instruction (chapter 1). Chapters 2, 3, 4, and 5 give information for teaching reading for meaning in a flexible and enjoyable way using a variety of materials. Chapters 6, 7, and 8 provide techniques for bringing writing into instruction, and have information to guide you in teaching the writing process.

Chapter 9 will stimulate your interest in speaking and listening as vehicles for instruction. Chapter 10 introduces mini-lessons and has activities for teaching a variety of skills including phonics, idea relationships (main idea and details, comparison and contrast, cause and effect), learning-style awareness, and study skills.

To tie it all together, chapter 11 suggests how to organize themes and describes three sample theme projects. By working on themes, students can integrate reading, writing, speaking, and listening as they explore and act on issues that are important to them.

Reading This Book

The authors of this book are experienced and successful practitioners. Here, they share what and how they teach, ways they organize activities, the ways teachers and students speak, and ways students form small groups and learning pairs during instruction. They put concepts to use to provide practical and effective vehicles for learning.

As you go through this book, you may find what you need to solve a particular problem in the general description of an activity. Or, as you read through an activity, you may find a specific technique or way to proceed, opening up a new direction for you in your teaching. That experience is in keeping with whole language. In exploring instruction that is layered and rich with detail, you can discover what is important and meaningful to you.

This book has an array of ideas that you can bring into instruction to stimulate and expand learning. We hope that you find it informative and enjoyable.

Betty Aderman, Editor

CHAPTER 1 PLANNING AND DESIGNING INSTRUCTION*

> "I never got attention in school and I didn't learn to read and write so I get pretty scared sometimes to speak my mind because it will show. Now my boy is in school and I can't tell if they pay attention to him or not. I'm not going to let it happen to him the way they did me." *An adult learner.*

> "It's not just reading and writing I want. I want to understand all those words people use and all the things they talk about. It starts there, in words and letters, but it goes further on." *An adult learner.*

Taking the desires of adult learners and your knowledge as an educator and using them to mold good educational experiences is a large responsibility. Deciding what to teach and how to teach it is challenging, but because it is the heart of our craft, it can also be the most dynamic and inspiring facet of our work.

In the process of planning and organizing instruction there are many questions to ask and factors to balance. How many adult learners do you have? At what levels are they? What do they want to learn? What are their learning styles? What can you teach them? How long is each session and how many weeks will the class run? Should students work individually? In small groups? In pairs? Do others have input into curriculum planning or will you be responsible for designing your own instruction with your students?

The information that follows is a guide to planning and designing instruction with flexibility and creativity. You and your students can use, adapt, and mold it to your circumstances.

To shape instruction that fits students' needs and interests, teachers and students participate together in the planning process. In this chapter, you'll find suggestions for planning instruction with your students and designing student-oriented instruction.

---

* Mallory Clarke contributed many of the ideas in this chapter and the photocopy masters.

Planning Instruction

In planning, students' personal goals are interwoven with the instructional choices that are available to you. Involving students in the planning process is crucial since they have the most to gain or lose from planning decisions.

Process:
- Get to know your students
- Discover students' goals
- Develop learning contracts

Get to know your students

Students are your most important resource for making planning decisions in the two phases of initial assessment: before placement and immediately after instruction begins. Successful planning and goal setting depend on finding answers to the following kinds of questions:

Where do the adult learners already use reading and writing in their lives?

Where would they like to be able to use it?

What do the adult learners already know about reading and writing?

What skills in reading and writing do they have?

What are their oral communication skills? Group skills? Interpersonal skills? Self-management skills?

How do they learn new things? Think critically? Think creatively?

How strong is their self-esteem?

What do the adult learners know about themselves as learners?

What are their preferred learning styles?

What are the adult learners' future goals?

What are they most interested in studying and discussing?

What have their past experiences with education been like?

What barriers do they need to overcome to continue their education?

Discover students' goals

By observing and talking with students you can help them clarify their goals and expectations. Students may need to know that a goal is something they want to be able to do. By sorting large goals into manageable pieces, they can achieve many short-term goals on the way to their long-term goals. With clear goals, you and your students can make long-range plans that will cover most of the time you have together. Together, you can make short-term plans for the steps along the way.

Goals are built on strengths and skills. Identifying what they already know and can do gives students a base for thinking about what they want to know and learn to do.

Use questionnaires and checklists. These are helpful tools for providing focus, stimulating discussion, and uncovering information to set both personal goals and goals for gaining new skills through instruction.

Using a personal goals questionnaire, students can articulate goals that relate instruction to various areas of their lives. (See the Personal Goals Questionnaire on page 13.)

A skills and goals checklist can help students review and preview skills attainable through instruction. (See the Skills and Goals Checklist on page 14.) The checklist should reflect the curriculum as well as the skill levels of students.

Personal Goals Questionnaire

Name _____   Class _____   Date _____

How do you use reading in your life?   How do you want to use reading?

Home	
Children	
Transportation	
Work	
Fun	
Other	

How do you use writing in your life?   How do you want to use writing?

Home	
Children	
Transportation	
Work	
Fun	
Other	

Skills and Goals Checklist

Directions: For each item, check (✓) *Strength* if you do it well; check (✓) *Goal* if you plan to work on it.

Reading

Strength	Goal	
____	____	Enjoy reading
____	____	Understand what I read
____	____	Know the sounds of letters
____	____	Read punctuation
____	____	Read aloud
____	____	Read silently
		Read different kinds of materials
____	____	poetry
____	____	fiction
____	____	nonfiction
____	____	newspapers
____	____	textbooks
____	____	other:
____	____	Find information
____	____	Predict what comes next
____	____	Know what to do if I have trouble
____	____	Sound out unfamiliar words
____	____	Guess the meaning of new words
____	____	Learn new vocabulary words
____	____	Use alphabetical order to find information
____	____	Use the dictionary
____	____	Remember what I read
____	____	Other:

Listening

Strength	Goal	
____	____	Understand what people say
____	____	Let people know that I understand
____	____	Let people know if I don't understand
____	____	Figure out what the conversation is about so I can add to it
____	____	Decide what I think about what people are saying
____	____	Understand directions the first or second time
____	____	Understand body language and tone of voice
____	____	Remember what people say
____	____	Take notes while I'm listening

Writing

Strength	Goal	
____	____	Enjoy writing
____	____	Have ideas to write about
____	____	Express myself in writing
____	____	Write letters of the alphabet
____	____	Write words
		Write for different reasons
____	____	make lists and write notes
____	____	write about myself
____	____	fill out forms
____	____	get my thoughts in order
____	____	say what I think and know
____	____	convince people of my ideas
____	____	take notes on what I hear
____	____	write letters
____	____	Write a lot at one sitting
____	____	Make my ideas fit together
____	____	Write more than one draft
____	____	Change ideas around
____	____	Use feedback from others to improve my writing
____	____	Give useful feedback to others
____	____	Make my paragraphs about a single idea
____	____	Proofread my own work
____	____	Spell most words correctly
____	____	Use punctuation correctly
____	____	Use formal English grammar
____	____	Use others to help proofread my writing
____	____	Other:

Speaking

Strength	Goal	
____	____	Speak clearly
____	____	Check that I've been understood
____	____	Know things to do to help people understand me
____	____	Encourage other people to speak
____	____	Know when to speak up and when to stay quiet
____	____	Talk in front of a group
____	____	Connect what I say to the topic
____	____	Organize my ideas when I talk
____	____	Ask questions to make things clearer
____	____	Use eye contact
____	____	Use formal English when it's appropriate

Develop learning contracts

A student learning contract for a specified period of instruction is one way to help students identify specific learning goals for themselves. (See the Student Learning Contract on page 16.) If students keep the contract up-to-date by reviewing and revising it at regular intervals, it acts as a guide for planning. Some contracts cover an entire course of instruction, while others cover shorter spans or even a single session.

Learning contracts help adult learners realize their own power and control over the learning process. By making a learning plan, you and your students develop shared expectations for instruction. Students talk about what they want to learn. You suggest ways to learn and introduce some of the vocabulary of instruction. Together you negotiate what each of you will contribute to the plan.

Here is an example of a developing reader contracting with her teacher:

Teacher: What are your general goals this time?

Student: I want to graduate to the next level and write my autobiography.

Teacher: Do you get a chance to read outside of class?

Student: I could read to my daughter.

Teacher: Reading aloud is a good way to get the rhythms of reading. You might also want to read about people's lives to see how other people have written biographies and autobiographies.

Student: But I need to read better so I remember what I read.

Teacher: There are strategies we can practice that help you think about what you're reading. That helps you remember. You can take notes, too.

Student: I can write to help me read.

Teacher: And I can read your autobiography when you write it.

Here, an advanced GED student contracts with his teacher:

Student: In writing, I need to practice essay writing and formal grammar.

Teacher: I'll make a list of essay topics for you and plan some lessons in grammar for the whole class.

Student: I want to get into the Culinary Arts program at the community college. I need to pass a test to get in and then read textbooks in those classes.

Teacher: Reading newspapers and textbooks will sharpen your reading skills. You can learn test-taking skills by doing practice tests and by learning techniques and strategies for passing tests. I can bring in some books on test taking. You could teach a lesson on test taking to the rest of the class.

Student: It all sounds good. But I'm not so sure about teaching the class.

Teacher: We can decide that later.

Student Learning Contract

Name _____   Dates: from _____ to _____

Teacher _____   Class _____

1. What are my general goals for this time period? _____

_____

2. Goals for reading:

    What am I going to work on? _____

    _____

    How am I going to do it? _____

    _____

    What will the teacher do to help me? _____

    _____

3. Goals for writing:

    What am I going to work on? _____

    _____

    How am I going to do it? _____

    _____

    What will the teacher do to help me? _____

    _____

4. Goals for speaking and listening:

    What am I going to work on? _____

    _____

    How am I going to do it? _____

    _____

    What will the teacher do to help me? _____

    _____

5. What is my goal for attendance? _____

_____

6. How will I check that I'm making progress toward my goals? _____

_____

Designing Student-Oriented Instruction

Planning involves thinking about an entire course of instruction. This includes thinking about a series of sessions, the arrangement of activities within a session, and each activity itself. The following are considerations for designing effective instruction.

Considerations:

Vary the activities
Create a collaborative atmosphere
Make the materials matter
Organize the activities
Provide for varied goals and needs
Make a long-range plan

Vary the activities

In some programs, teachers have a set curriculum and assigned core texts. In others, teachers design their own curriculum and use a variety of texts. The activities described below can fit into any curriculum to enliven instruction and make learning meaningful and personal.

Sustained silent reading. A regular period of time set aside for students to read what they like. You read silently also.

Reading activity. Instruction in reading for meaning that usually includes preparing to read, reading, and processing what was read.

Journal writing. Opportunities to write unstructured, unedited thoughts on topics chosen by students or that you've suggested. You can read and respond to your students' journals. But responses need to focus on content, ignoring style and writing mechanics.

Writing activity. One of a series of activities that may or may not lead to a finished writing product, but that includes some of the many stages writers go through.

Spoken-language activity. An activity that draws on students' skills in listening and speaking so they can experience facets of language and communication that contribute to and develop from reading and writing. These may include group discussions, role plays, speeches, and talking about language.

Mini-lesson. A brief, frequently occurring activity during which any specific skill or aspect of language and communication is taught. Mini-lessons can relate to past, present, or future work that students do in other activities. Because mini-lessons are self-contained activities, they do not interrupt the focus on communication during reading, writing, or discussion. A mini-lesson can provide a break in routine or a transition from individual to group work.

Teachable moments. Unanticipated moments when learners are open to guidance from you. By pointing out new skills being practiced and showing students how to solve problems that arise during the session, you can help your students become aware of their thinking and gain control of skills and strategies. You need to plan how you will be available during activities so you can notice and respond to teachable moments.

Theme projects. A series of activities in which students investigate and act on issues that they choose to work on because they find the issues interesting and important. Themes involve reading, writing, speaking, and listening.

Homework. Simple assignments that allow students to succeed when working alone. These assignments can be for review or practice, or for research in the community in preparation for theme projects.

Assessment. An important part of the planning process that continues throughout instruction. When students note what they learned, what they enjoyed, and what they want to do more of, they are encouraged to reflect on their own learning and provide direction for future planning. By reflecting on the session and how learners responded, you can decide what to prepare as a follow-up as well as what changes to make.

Create a collaborative atmosphere

Teachers and learners are partners in instruction. Thinking of students as co-teachers and of teachers as co-learners provides the basis for effective instruction. Adult students have a wealth of expertise and knowledge, and they can operate well as instructors for each other, for the group as a whole, and for you. When students are encouraged to help shape the class, contribute their ideas, and take responsibility for each others' learning, the work of instruction becomes a shared venture, and the class becomes more democratic. The suggestions that follow help establish a collaborative atmosphere.

Start where the students are. Incorporating the adult learners' experiences into teaching activities shows respect for their knowledge, culture, and skills. It also helps them learn. When you acknowledge and explore what adult learners already know about a topic, you activate their memories and at the same time help prepare others in the group who might not have a strong background on that particular topic. Once this base is built, learning can move forward to cover new ground.

Teach from the students' points of view. When students' own experiences, cultures, and knowledge have been welcomed into the learning process, they become more open to new experiences. New topics or subjects that students associate with intimidating and negative educational experiences in the past become interesting to them when they feel that what they already know is valued, when they have a shared comfort with each other as a community of learners, and when they know they are accepted by their teacher.

One important way to incorporate the students' points of view into teaching is to use examples from their lives rather than relying on examples in texts. For example, you can demonstrate how to keep a journal using an actual journal of a past student (with the student's permission). You can create exercises using sentences about events and people familiar to students.

To show how writing changes through the phases of the writing process, you can start with two versions of a letter you write to students about what teaching them means to you.

Provide useful practice. Have students practice and apply new skills in ways students want to use them. To practice ways to remember what was read, use a reading passage that students want to remember. For students in a GED program, you can prepare passages that detail the steps to apply for the GED test or to get into a community college program. To practice writing business letters, suggest that students actually write to companies that have sold them inadequate goods, to ask for replacements or refunds. To practice assertive verbal communication, in addition to in-class role plays, you can invite a police officer in to explain the police force's internal review process for citizen complaints. Assign students to observe the officer's verbal behavior and the verbal behavior of the class.

Help students think about how they learn. Students can learn in ways that are most efficient for them if they become aware of their preferred learning styles. They can try out new approaches, knowing that they might feel awkward at first. By helping students reflect on their own thinking processes (called metacognition), you help students learn to pay attention to their thinking. By talking about the thinking they do to try to understand a message or make themselves understood, students can learn to identify problems they are having and develop strategies to deal with them.

Make the materials matter

Students learning to read and write need a wide variety of meaningful and purposeful reading materials. With relevant materials, students can experience many different aspects of reading and writing. Students also need specific practice materials that are useful and engaging. Programs and teachers need to continuously acquire and produce new materials.

No single series or book should be the sole resource for instruction. A variety of materials is essential for effective instruction and meaningful learning. General reading materials, adult literacy publishers' materials, teacher-made materials, and student-made materials are all useful resources.

General reading materials. Newspaper clippings, books, magazines, pamphlets, and junk mail that you and your students bring to class are all valuable. You can also use community resources to develop a pool of materials sorted by topic and reading level. Building a good collection takes time and should be the shared responsibility of the program and the individual teachers. If you have access to a library, you can use the library's interstate lending system, newspaper archives, computerized search systems, and collections of art, music, film, and videos.

Adult literacy publishers' materials. These include instructional series to develop reading and writing skills, skill practice books, reading anthologies, and high-interest, low-difficulty newspapers and books. Some of the materials have teacher's guides or teacher's editions that provide suggestions and activities. Teachers can examine these materials at the library, by contacting publishers for free catalogs, and by browsing through publishers' exhibits at conferences.

Teacher-made materials. Teacher-made materials are an excellent way to fill the need for appropriate materials. Since you, more than anyone, are aware of the needs and interests of your students, you can tailor your materials to the specific requirements of an activity you design. For example, you can prepare materials that use vocabulary words students have been working on. You can prepare readings with information on specific topics that you and your students have been talking about. You can create materials in advance or on the spot. You can make published materials more readable by shortening or simplifying them to meet your students' needs. Libraries, state departments of education, the U.S. Department of Education (Division of Adult Education and Literacy), and ERIC (Educational Resources and Information Center) are all sources for information on developing curriculum, activities, and materials.

Reading materials

Passages on topics brought up in class

Passages adding information to a previous discussion

Newspaper articles adapted or rewritten to a lower level

Passages that develop the main ideas of difficult texts

Correspondence between students and teachers

Materials to explore concepts

Stick-figure diagrams to teach grammar usage and written dialogue

Description cards with information on them for a role play

Sentence strips for playing with the organization of ideas

Envelopes containing word cards to use in categorizing

Materials to make published reading selections more accessible

Introductions to provide background information

Prereading questions about a text for students to answer

Postreading questions to help students personally connect to what they read and share their understandings

Exercises and games for skill practice

Reading examples using students' names and life circumstances

Cloze exercises: published or student-written passages in which you put blanks for words or letters that students fill in

Games like Concentration or poker, using word or letter cards

Passages with specific errors for students to proofread

Student-made materials. Students of all levels can create materials. Non-proficient writers can use invented spelling or even drawing to create materials. Students' spoken statements can be turned into reading material by writing down what the student says. The technique to produce reading material from students' spoken language is called the language experience approach (LEA).

Reading materials

Passages created by students

Materials (pamphlets, bills, notices) brought from home, children's schools, or work

Freewriting or first drafts for comment

Desktop-published student writing

Materials to explore concepts

Maps of a familiar neighborhood or layouts of buildings

Diagrams or illustrations developed to depict experiences or ideas

Dialogues to present aspects of communication

Exercises for skill practice

Student-generated words, sentences, and paragraphs

Student-made test questions

Organize the activities

Planning which activities to provide in a session and how to organize activities across sessions involves considerations of timing, variety, and opportunities to deepen and broaden learning over time. The suggestions that follow are useful for planning activities within a session.

Create a rhythm. It is very important to have a pattern of activity that keeps adult learners engaged. Some work is introspective, reflective, and quiet. Other work is active, interactive, and noisy. Creating a rhythm that moves from one to the other without abrupt or awkward transitions is a key to building and maintaining momentum. Focused studying needs to be balanced with the more relaxed practice of familiar concepts. Learning should balance with practice, struggle with success. You should also be aware of the amount of mental work being done in relation to physical movement, since most students need to do both to stay alert.

Vary types of reading and writing. Reading materials and writing tasks need to be varied in length and difficulty. Brief materials enable adult learners to complete a task in one session. Other materials might require several sessions. When students are trying an activity or skill for the first time, easy materials are best. More difficult materials are appropriate when students are practicing a skill or developing strategies for handling materials that present a challenge to them. Materials should also vary by topic and type of text. Variety expands learners' repertoires and provides the flexibility needed for reading and writing in daily life.

Spiral the activities. Most skills, strategies, or bodies of knowledge cannot be grasped at one sitting. Students must revisit a subject many times to make it theirs. Each time a subject is revisited you can add new dimensions, require greater mastery, or expand the information explored. This process of circling back to study a subject and addressing it at a slightly higher level is called spiraling.

Schedule time for each activity. The better you know your students, the easier it is to estimate how long an activity will take. Even if the estimate is not entirely accurate, it is helpful to have an approximate time frame in mind. Beginning teachers often find it difficult to fill the time allotted, while teachers with more experience find that there is rarely enough time. In any case, it is better to plan too many activities, in case a particular activity does not work out or takes less time than you expected.

It is also helpful to plan flexible activities for the beginning and the end of the class, since some learners may need to arrive late or leave early. Some teachers rotate beginning and ending activities, such as sustained silent reading, journal writing, or independent work, so that students who must come late or leave early can participate in the activities at least part of the time.

Make a general session plan. To provide continuity, arrange activities in a format for a typical session. Together, the activities should provide for reading, writing, speaking, and listening to occur within the session. The actual sequence of activities often involves a mix of old and new business.

Suggested Session Format	Time
Opening activity	brief
Homework review	varied
Continuing activity (ongoing from previous sessions)	extended
New challenge	varied
Closing activity	varied
Evaluation and homework assignment	brief

Provide for varied goals and needs

Planning involves meeting the varied goals and needs of learners in an atmosphere of shared learning. The suggestions that follow can help you incorporate learners' differences in planning.

Provide opportunities for collaborative learning. There are many benefits to collaboration and cooperation. When students work together in pairs or in small groups, they have the chance to see things from several viewpoints, learn from other adults like themselves, negotiate reading and writing as social acts, and gain experience in problem solving, group effectiveness, and communication. Mutual help prepares students for the kinds of teaching and learning that goes on in other areas of their lives.

Balance learning styles called for in activities. Most activities reward a particular learning style because they involve only one learning mode: reading and writing, listening and speaking, or visualizing and manipulating. Keeping track of the learning modes needed for each activity helps assure a balance of different types of activities. As much as possible, teach to learners' strengths while giving them chances to practice other styles and combinations.

Create subgroups. Small groups of students can work together to explore topics of interest and improve their reading and writing skills. Working in subgroups provides more intense learning opportunities and accommodates various learning styles.

Pairs can read to each other, give each other feedback on their writing, or help each other with spelling or vocabulary drills. In a three-person group, one student can be assigned as the facilitator to keep the group on task and record group decisions. Small groups of four or five can collaborate to complete tasks, do research, or come to consensus on issues. Groups can also be formed of those students who need more work on a specific skill.

Usually, groupings are heterogeneous to allow adult learners to learn from each other, but a group can be formed of students at a similar level. Some teachers report better attendance and retention when larger classes have permanent subgroups for various activities.

Mixed-level classes. All classes are mixed-level to some extent, since adult learners read and write with different degrees of competency. However, sometimes a single class serves all students in a given location. Effective instruction of a mixed-level class involves using materials with a range of difficulty levels, using audiotapes for lower-level readers, and having students read difficult texts in pairs. You can have advanced students learn by teaching the rest of the class, reading aloud to others who take notes, and writing summaries for other students to read. Time needs to be devoted to mini-lessons with one subgroup while students at other levels do collaborative or independent work. Whole-class discussions and presentations are also important to create unity. Using nonprint media in whole-class activities helps all members of the class participate fully.

Make a long-range plan

Taking into account students' goals and your tools for instruction, you can make a long-range plan. Long-range plans are flexible guides that change over time. The timeline for plans varies. Some teachers make a monthlong plan; others make longer plans. Long-range planning questions include:

What goals do most of the students have in common?

What skills can benefit most of the students?

What are the students' reading levels?

What subgroups can be formed from shared needs or interests?

What are some high-interest topics for possible themes?

What are possible special events or trips?

What is the overall length of time we have together?

What is the time available for each session?

How are activities arranged in a session?

CHAPTER 2 BRIDGES TO READING

We learn by connecting something new to what we already know. We often think of prior knowledge in terms of knowing about content or subject matter. This is a vital form of knowledge, but two other kinds of knowledge are also needed: knowing how to make meaning and knowing how to communicate with language.

Making meaning is a mental process that involves seeking out, interpreting, and acting on clues in our environment. To help adult learners realize that reading is a meaning-making activity, we can make the connection between reading print and other kinds of "reading" we do.

Reading is something we all do. We read each other's moods, we read the clouds looking for rain, and, because we are human beings trying to make sense of our world, we are always reading into things. Sometimes we misread, and sometimes we know that we haven't understood. This, too, is a vital part of making meaning.

One way to help students become aware of the ways they make meaning is to read pictures. Talking about our responses to pictures and what we think they mean can lay the groundwork for the kinds of thinking and attitudes we want students to bring to reading. Talking about how an artist created a piece that other people can or cannot make sense of can give helpful ideas about communicating as a writer.

Knowledge about language is also needed. Nearly all adults know spoken language. We know how to use language in different ways for different purposes: to learn, remember, convince, and entertain. And we know how language works: as patterns within patterns, from words in order to single statements, whole stories, and arguments. This knowledge is tapped and expanded when we learn to read and write.

The language experience approach (LEA) is a powerful and flexible technique to connect speaking to reading and writing. It helps students use their knowledge of spoken language for learning to read and write and creating a variety of reading materials.

This chapter provides activities for reading pictures and using the language experience approach.

Reading It Like a Book

Students can become aware of the reading process by viewing and talking about pictures in a way that parallels the way they read text.

Purpose: To help students understand that reading, like viewing, is a process by which we create meaning.

Process:
Preview
View
Postview

Materials: Several reproductions of paintings or photographs. Select pictures that have an underlying relationship, such as pictures by the same artist or pictures with the same subject matter.

Preview

Introduce the pictures to students. Discuss content, colors, or any aspects that are familiar to the students. Set a purpose for looking at the pictures.

Teacher: Look at the pictures to understand what the artist is saying. Think about how you feel and what the artist did that makes you feel that way. Compare the pictures. How are they the same or different from each other?

View

Ask students to examine the pictures and talk about them as they look.

Postview

Invite students to share their responses or ideas. Discuss how viewing is similar to reading. Close the activity by reading or writing, perhaps choosing a reading selection on the same topic as the pictures. If you have been comparing and contrasting pictures, you might choose a reading selection that is built on comparison. In writing, students may describe a picture or express feelings evoked by a picture.

Teacher: Artists create a visual message just as authors create a written message. Viewers recognize patterns in lines and colors. There are also patterns in what we read. A story and an article have their own distinct patterns. Viewers have ideas, feelings, and opinions about pictures. Similarly, readers react to what they are reading. Just as you can read the pictures, you can use the same process of making meaning to read and write words.

Sample: Reading It Like a Book
Reading Pictures

To explore how to read for meaning, students compared two postcard art reproductions. Then the class read a poem that compared two images.

Purpose: To help students move past their preoccupation with decoding and gain confidence in their ability to read for meaning.

Materials: Picture postcards on the same topic by different artists.

I am the Resurrection and the Life, by Harvey Dunn, South Dakota Art Museum Collection, Brookings, South Dakota.

Queena Stovall, *Swing Low, Sweet Chariot,* 1953, oil on canvas, 28 x 40 in. Courtesy of Maier Museum of Art, Randolph-Macon Woman's College, Lynchburg, Virginia.

Preview

Each student took one of two postcards. Then they formed pairs so that each pair had both pictures.

Teacher: These two pictures are by two different painters. Both painted scenes from daily life. They both lived at about the same time, but their scenes are very different. Harvey Dunn (1884–1952) painted scenes of pioneer life on the Dakota prairie. Queena Stovall (1888–1980) painted scenes of rural life in Virginia. Dunn's work is realistic and raw. He shows how hard prairie life was. Stovall's work is homey and warm, showing life in loving detail.

View

In pairs, students looked at and talked about the pictures. Then the whole group reconvened to discuss their impressions.

Teacher: Tell me some things you see in these pictures.

Student: Both pictures show people at a funeral.

Student: The *Swing Low* picture looks good. Everybody is dressed up. There's lots of flowers.

Teacher: OK. Let's look at some differences in these paintings. What did the artists do that makes them very different funeral scenes?

Students: Well, in *Swing Low* it's sad, but it's peaceful and pretty. The other picture feels like it's windy and cold. It looks like those people are about to blow away.

Teacher: Look at what the artists did. They painted the grass differently. Queena Stovall made the grass look peaceful by painting it smoothly. But Harvey Dunn put brush lines in his picture so it looks like grass blowing in the wind. It's interesting that both pictures are about the same thing, but they look so different and make you feel so different when you see them.

What you did was read the paintings. You used what you already know to understand what you were looking at. You didn't think about every little brush stroke, but you went after the meanings, what the paintings were about. That's what you want to do when you read. And when you write, you do the same thing that the artists did. You decide what you want to write about and what to put in your writing so your readers get the picture you want them to have.

Let's read this poem together. It's not about a funeral, but it is about two different types of weather. The writer compared two pictures he saw in his mind. See if you like the poem or not. Then we'll talk about what the poem is about, how we felt when we read it, and what the author did that made us feel that way.

Ever Notice

Ever notice how it's always quiet
When it snows
Snow descends so unobtrusively
Bringing with it clouds of light
Even on a dismal day
And it makes its entrance so serenely

Ever notice
How unlike rain, which often has
A thunderous introduction
Snow doesn't seem to need
　a round of applause
Before taking the stage

Ever notice

From *I Wanna Be the Kinda Father My Mother Was*, by Omanii Abdullah, New Readers Press, 1993.

Using the Language Experience Approach

The language experience approach (LEA) allows students to create their own reading materials by speaking and having someone write down what they say. LEA is useful whenever speaking rather than writing helps composition. It is especially valuable for new readers and writers. Here is a description of the general technique and suggested uses for it in instruction.

Purpose: To help students use their spoken-language skills to create interesting reading materials and to learn new information.

Materials: Chalkboard or flip chart, a computer (optional), a copy machine (optional), stimulus object (optional).

Process:

- Set up
- Record
- Use

Set up

Designate a scribe and choose a stimulus. A stimulus is something students see, read, or listen to that stimulates expression.

Record

The scribe writes down what the student says. Watching the scribe write as they speak allows students to see the transfer of speech to writing and helps students slow the flow of speech so it approximates the rhythms of writing. The scribe can also prompt the student to continue creating text by asking: What else happened? What is the main thing you want people to know? How do you want this to end?

When recording, the scribe uses correct spelling and punctuation. The scribe may make minor changes to standardize usage, but this is done only to translate spoken language into written language, not to tamper with the author's voice or meaning. The scribe prepares a readable copy of the dictation and returns it to the student who uses it like any reading material.

Use

The following are some suggested uses for LEA in reading instruction.

Reading for meaning. LEA allows all students to produce interesting materials that they can read. Because the language and ideas are their own, students can quickly learn to read their own LEA material fluently and with understanding and enjoyment. At more advanced levels, LEA material is useful for trying out new comprehension skills. Students can successfully locate information in the text, summarize, or state the main idea when the reading selection is one that they have produced.

Word study. At early stages of reading, students' spoken-language vocabularies are larger than their sight word vocabularies, so LEA materials are an excellent source of sight words for word study. Students choose words from their passages to put on word cards for later practice.

Responding to reading. After reading or listening to a selection, you can record students' responses and check for comprehension. You can record students' statements about what the selection told them, what they found interesting, and what they thought of the piece.

Learning new information. Using their own words, students can create texts to learn new ideas, facts, vocabulary, and grammatical structures. They can create reference books, simplified versions of difficult texts, or texts from information presented to them.

Note: LEA can be used with groups in a variety of ways: to make lists of group brainstorming, to compose a group letter or story, and to record group decisions for sharing with the whole class. A whole class can compose a single composition. In a variation, each student can compose individually in a group setting. On each turn, every person responds in his or her own way to a given prompt. The scribe keeps track of who says what and puts together all the statements a person has made to create each person's complete text.

These are three simple ground rules for composing in a group LEA:

- Provide a prearranged turn-taking order.
- Encourage all students to use their turn.
- Keep each turn short—one or two statements.

Sample: Using the Language Experience Approach
Using LEA with a New Reader

By using LEA, a teacher helped a student correspond with his sons who had gone away to college. Here he wrote the first of many letters.

Purpose: To help a new reader communicate in print.

Set up

Teacher: Carl, you say you want to write letters to your boys. Have you thought about what you'd like to say in a letter?
Student: I know it exactly. I want to say, "Dear Boys, Daddy loves you."
Teacher: Can you write that?
Student: No, I can't write.
Teacher: Can you write any words?
Student: I don't think so.
Teacher: You wrote the letter in your mind, so I'll write it on paper.
Student: But I want it to be in my handwriting.
Teacher: OK. After I write it, you take it home and copy it over.

Record

Teacher: OK. Say it again and I'll write it down.
Student: "Dear Boys, Daddy loves you."
Teacher: Do you want to sign it "Love, Dad"?
Student: No, I want "Love, Carl." Those boys need to know their daddy can sign his name.

Dear Boys,
Daddy loves you.
                 Love, Carl

(Teacher)

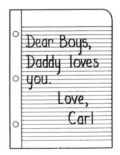

(Student)

The next session, Carl brought in a nicely copied letter and read it to the teacher. He also brought a stamp, and together they prepared the envelope.

Use

Over a two-year period, the student learned to read and write mostly by writing letters to his sons and reading the letters he got from them.

Sample: Using the Language Experience Approach
Using LEA to Learn New Content

To help prepare for a written driver's test, a group of mixed-level students created a simplified version of the state driver's manual. Through LEA, their ability to read the manual improved, and they learned the information they needed to pass the test. During each session they focused on a different section of the manual. The topic for this meeting was "passing."

Purpose: To help students learn new information and create a text they could study.

Materials: Copies of the state driver's manual, a chalkboard or flip chart, student notebooks.

Set up

The teacher introduced the topic, handed out driver's manuals to the group, and asked questions to find out what students already knew.

Teacher: What do you know about passing another car? I'll list what you say on the board.

Students: You can't pass on a solid yellow line. Don't pass on a hill. Don't pass a bunch of traffic.

Teacher: You know a lot already. Let's see what else the manual says.

To make sure that the information in the text was available to all students regardless of their reading level, the teacher and some of the students took turns reading aloud from the section on passing while the other students followed along silently.

Record

To prepare the text, the teacher asked students to recall in their own words what they read. She put what they said on the board. This technique was useful for a number of reasons: It allowed the group to make sure that everyone understood the information, it helped students learn the information and vocabulary, and it provided a text that all the students could read because they had created it together.

Teacher: Let's go around the group. Each person say one important thing to remember about passing. Listen to each other. If you are not sure the information is right, we'll flag it and check the manual.

Use

Teacher: Now let's read what we've got on the board to make sure it says what we want. Then you can copy the section about passing from the board into your notebooks to have it for study and review.

CHAPTER 3 THE READING PROCESS

Learning to read effectively helps students achieve the fundamental goal of becoming independent readers and writers. Students can develop independence in a variety of ways. They can read often, read a wide variety of materials, take charge of their own reading, and read for understanding as an act of genuine communication.

As students become independent readers, they engage in reading as a process that involves prereading, reading, and postreading. Each phase is important to comprehension; each requires active participation. In prereading, we identify what we already know about a subject and what we need to know to build a base for understanding. We set a goal or purpose for reading. In reading, our goals and interest in the subject guide us to make meaning from what we read despite rough spots caused by unfamiliar words or difficult sentences. In postreading, we relate what we learned to what we already knew. We strengthen previously held ideas and develop new ones.

This chapter presents basic techniques to help students learn to use the reading process effectively. These techniques are the Directed Reading Activity, Modeling Reading, Assisted Reading, Sustained Silent Reading, and Word Recognition Strategies. The following chart shows how each technique fits within the reading process.

Basic Techniques to Promote Reading for Meaning			
Instructional Technique	Prereading	Reading	Postreading
Directed Reading Activity	gather prior knowledge preview set purpose predict	read all or section	discuss check prediction
Modeling Reading	think aloud	read and think aloud	discuss and review
Assisted Reading		teacher and student briefly read aloud difficult section	
Word Recognition Strategies		use context and word-part clues	
Sustained Silent Reading	select material	read silently	comment informally

Conducting a Directed Reading Activity (DRA)

A Directed Reading Activity (DRA) provides the basic format for teaching the reading process. Structuring the reading activity according to prereading, reading, and postreading phases of the reading process helps students internalize the reading process over time. At first, the teacher conducts the activity, but as students become more familiar with the reading process, they can take charge of their own learning. In pairs or small groups, students can choose reading selections, prepare for reading, check for understanding during reading, and discuss afterward what they gained from reading.

A reading planning guide can be used to plan a reading activity. (See the Teacher's Guide for Planning a Reading Activity on page 36.) A reader's guide can help students move through each phase of the reading process. (See the Reader's Guide on page 37.)

Purpose: To help students use the reading process to read for meaning.

Materials: Any relevant reading selection that students can read with some assistance if necessary.

Process:

| Prereading |
| Reading |
| Postreading |

Prereading

The prereading phase sets the stage for reading. This phase is essential to achieving active reading. The more energy you and your students devote to prereading, the better the students will be able to understand and appreciate what they read. In prereading, you introduce the reading selection so that students know what the topic is, and why you chose it. Then, help students identify what they already know and learn what they need to know so they can understand the subject matter and the language in the selection. They should then preview the text to understand how the information is laid out and to anticipate difficulties. They should also set a purpose for reading.

These are some common practices to prepare students for reading:

Encourage students to recall what they already know about the topic.

Provide background information that students may need.

Identify new vocabulary.

Provide specific instruction in a needed skill.

Alert students to potential tough spots in the passage.

Have students predict what they will find as they read.

Reading

Students read the selection, guided by ideas presented in the prereading phase. Encourage silent reading. New readers may want to read aloud initially but should begin silent reading of short sections of text as soon as possible. Students may read on their own, in pairs, or in small groups.

If the text is difficult or long, you may want to use a variation of the DRA that is called the Directed Reading-Thinking Activity (DR-TA).* In a DR-TA, you divide the reading into sections. Look for naturally occurring sections, such as single paragraphs, information presented under a subheading, individual steps in a procedure, a change of scene, or the entrance of a new character in a story. For each section, ask students to predict what they expect to find. Then, to check for comprehension after each section is completed, students can discuss the differences between what they predicted and what they actually read. As students progress through the passage, their predictions should become more accurate, since the previous reading becomes part of their prior knowledge.

Postreading

Students respond to what they read. They give their reactions, feelings, and opinions. They relate the information to their own lives, and they integrate the information into their own prior knowledge. To react to what they read, students might say what they like, what they find interesting, what they agree and disagree with. To relate the reading to their lives, students might say how the information is useful to them, what they do, want to do, or could do related to the topic. To process the information, students can discuss how the reading met or differed from their expectations. They can talk about what they learned and what they'd like to know more about. In writing, students can expand on the ideas gained from reading. They can write down ideas they want to remember or write their own views. They can do follow-up activities to put into action the ideas they read, discussed, and wrote about.

* From *Directed Reading Maturity as a Cognitive Process,* by R. G. Stauffer, Harper and Row, 1969.

Sample: Conducting a Directed Reading Activity (DRA)

Engaging in the Reading Process

Here's how a teacher led a DRA using a reading selection from a reading instruction book. She chose the selection because it had an interesting topic—handwriting.

To plan for the reading activity, the teacher made a list of words related to handwriting for students to identify. She then had each student write, "The quick brown fox jumped over the lazy dog," so they could analyze their handwriting. Then she divided the text into sections to make it easier to read. She also thought about which students to pair as reading partners.

Prereading

Teacher: You have all been doing a lot to improve your handwriting recently, so I thought you might be interested in reading a selection about handwriting. It's about what handwriting experts look for when they examine someone's handwriting. But first, write this sentence so we can have a sample of everyone's handwriting.

The teacher then handed out the four-paragraph reading selection on handwriting.

Handwriting

Everything we do tells other people something about who we are. Some people think that they can learn a lot about us by studying our handwriting. Sometimes these people hire handwriting experts. . . .

There are at least sixteen factors that a handwriting expert looks at when he studies handwriting. One factor is the slant of the letters. . . .

A second factor in studying handwriting is how the writing line goes. . . .

A third factor in studying handwriting is to note how big and wide the letters are. . . .

From Book 2 of the *Challenger* Adult Reading Series, by Corea Murphy, New Readers Press, 1985.

Teacher: Now, look at the title and read the first three sentences. What do you think people can learn from studying a person's handwriting? Who might want to hire a handwriting expert?

After a brief discussion, the teacher again directed the students to the text.

Teacher: Spend a little time looking over the reading again. Look at each paragraph. Read the first sentence of each paragraph. Try to get an idea of what the reading selection is about. What do you think we will find out from reading this selection?

Reading

Teacher: Now let's form pairs to read. We'll read the first paragraph together. Quickly look over the paragraph. Tell your partner what you think you will find in the paragraph. Then, read silently. When you finish, tell your partner what the paragraph was actually about. See if your partner found the same things. Then we'll all share what we read in the paragraph. We'll follow this procedure for all four paragraphs.

Postreading

Teacher: Now, everyone look at the sentence that you wrote before you started reading. Analyze your handwriting. Does your handwriting reveal the kind of person you are? Do you agree with what you read?

Teacher's Guide for Planning a Reading Activity

Student(s) _____   Date _____

Reading Selection _____

Directions: List what you want to ask or tell your students to guide them through the reading selection.

Prereading

1. How will I encourage students to think about what they already know?

2. What background information will I provide?

3. What new vocabulary or skill instruction will I provide?

4. When should students predict what they will read?

5. How will students set a purpose for reading?

Reading

1. What will the students read (whole selection, sections)?

2. Will the students read silently or aloud?

3. Who will the students share with as they read (pairs, groups, teacher)?

Postreading

1. What might the students learn?

2. What was expected or unexpected?

3. How can the students use the information?

4. Ideas for writing:

5. Additional reading:

6. Other activities:

Reader's Guide

Name _____ Date _____

Reading Selection _____

Directions: Answer the questions as you go through each part of the reading process.

Prereading

What do I already know about this subject? _____

_____

What do I think I will learn from reading this? _____

_____

Reading

How easy was it to read? _____

_____

How did I deal with difficult parts? _____

_____

What did I like about the reading? _____

_____

Who did I share my reading with? _____

_____

What information did I read? _____

_____

Postreading

What did I find out that I expected to learn? _____

_____

What did I find out that I did not expect? _____

_____

What new ideas do I have? _____

_____

What do I want to do with this information? _____

_____

Modeling Reading

Frequent modeling for students is a way they can learn how experienced readers and writers think and act. Modeling can be a reenactment of reading or writing to demonstrate behavior, or modeling can be actual reading or writing in the learners' presence. Either way, modeling works best when it is honest and shows the real, not an ideal. In this activity, the teacher shows students how to engage actively in reading.

Purpose: To demonstrate the reading process.

Materials: A reading selection that is somewhat difficult for students to read. Every student should have a copy of the selection.

Process:
- Preread aloud
- Read and think aloud
- Postread aloud and review

Preread aloud

Reading and thinking are usually internalized behaviors. To demonstrate them, you need to read aloud and say what you are thinking. Advise students to read along silently. Begin by surveying the selection. Comment on ideas you gain from the title and pictures, and words or phrases you notice. Mention a few things that you already know about the subject. Set a purpose for reading; say why you are reading and what you intend to gain.

Read and think aloud

Read a part of the passage aloud. Then, pause to share what is going through your mind. Comment on interesting ideas you read, things you don't agree with, or any awkward wording. State any personal connections you make as you read. If you are not sure of what something means, say so, and consider some possible meanings. Continue in this way—reading, pausing, and sharing your thinking as you read.

As you continue to read aloud, have students take a more active role. Instead of saying what you are thinking when you pause, ask students what they are thinking, what questions they have, or what they are learning.

Postread aloud and review

Discuss the whole selection. Share what you think and feel as a result of having read the piece. Relate new ideas to what you knew before. Review with students what they noticed about the reading process and what they learned from the demonstration.

Doing Assisted Reading

Reading along with an experienced reader, either a more advanced student or the teacher, can help students keep the thread of meaning. Assisted reading helps new readers experience fluent reading. In general, assisted reading can help students "over the hump" when they encounter a difficult section of text that jeopardizes comprehension. To help build students' confidence that they can read on their own, use assisted reading only occasionally and only for short periods (5–10 minutes).

Purpose: To help students through difficult text by reading with them.

Materials: A reading selection that is difficult for the student to read alone. If the assisted reading is a planned activity, each student should have a copy of the reading selection.

There are two variations of assisted reading. In echo reading, the teacher reads aloud, then the student reads aloud. In paired or duet reading,* the teacher and student read aloud together.

Echo Reading

Teacher: Let's read this together. I will read a sentence aloud. Then, you read the same sentence.

Reading. Increase the amount of text that is read at one time from a single sentence to two sentences, then a paragraph. Pause frequently to encourage the student to comment on what was just read as a way to help the student pay attention to meaning.

Paired Reading

Teacher: Read along with me. Try to keep up the pace as best you can.

Reading. Read aloud in unison. Set the pace and pull the student along. If the student falters, or misses a word, supply it, and ask the student to repeat it. Then, continue reading. When the student begins to read with fluency, lower your voice so that the student hears her own voice clearly. Gradually stop reading and allow the student to read alone. If the student begins to have difficulty, join in reading again until she regains confidence.

---

* From "Training Family and Friends as Adult Literacy Tutors," by J. Scoble, K. Topping, and C. Wigglesworth, in the *Journal of Reading,* International Reading Association, 1988.

Teaching Word Recognition Strategies

All adult learners occasionally encounter unknown words that block their ability to understand what they are reading. Sometimes they come upon a word that they do not recognize and they cannot proceed. At other times they realize that what they are reading has stopped making sense because they have misread a word. For these times, students need a strategy that helps them deal with the problem word and get back on track. The overall strategy is called reading for meaning.

Here are two word recognition strategies. One is for new and developing readers. The other is for more advanced readers.

Purpose: To teach students a strategy for dealing with difficult words that they encounter when reading.

A Strategy for New and Developing Readers: Context-Phonics-Context

New and developing readers usually know more words than they can recognize in print. These students often have difficulty with phonics. They can't sound out the word well enough to recognize it. To overcome this problem, teach students to use a combination of context and phonics clues.

Step 1: Context

Teacher: When you are reading along and you come to a word that you can't figure out, go back to the start of the sentence. Read to the unknown word, skip it, and read to the end of the sentence. Think about clues to the word that you can gain from the context of the rest of the sentence.

Step 2: Phonics

Teacher: Return to the unknown word and look at its first and last letters. Then, look for any other familiar parts. Think about clues to the word that you can gain from these letters. Now, try to guess the word using both the context and phonics.

Step 3: Context

Teacher: Read the entire sentence, including the word you've guessed. Does the word make sense in context? If so, continue. If not, look for more clues and try again.

A Strategy for More Advanced Readers: Context-Structure-Dictionary

Intermediate and advanced readers can usually sound out words, but may need additional clues to understand what they mean. To help students deal with new words, teach students to use first a combination of context and word-structure clues, and then to use the dictionary.

Step 1: Context

Teacher: When you encounter a new word, sound it out. Then, read the sentence in which the word appears. Think about clues to the word that you gain from the rest of the sentence. Try to guess what the word means. If your guess makes sense, read on.

Step 2: Structure

Teacher: If you cannot guess the word from the context, look at its structure. Are there any familiar prefixes or suffixes? What does the root mean? Try to guess what the word means by using what you've learned from the context and structure. If you can guess, read on.

Step 3: Dictionary

Teacher: If you can't guess a reasonable word from the context and structure, it's time to look the word up in a dictionary. Remember that what you've learned from context and structure can help you understand the dictionary definition.

Doing Sustained Silent Reading (SSR)

Providing students with frequent and regularly scheduled periods for reading on their own in class fosters independent reading and helps students develop lifelong reading habits. In Sustained Silent Reading (SSR)* students choose something to read silently for a short period of time (5–20 minutes). This is the only opportunity for many students to sit quietly just reading. It is important that you participate, too, in order to model actual reading for pleasure.

Many teachers schedule SSR just as the session begins so that students enter a quiet environment and start reading. However, if you have students whose schedule requires them to arrive late or leave early, you may want to alternate SSR between the beginning and end of sessions so that all students get a chance to participate.

Purpose: To provide a regular opportunity to read for pleasure.

Materials: A wide variety of materials so all learners can find something of interest that they can either read easily or at least browse through. Include a variety of magazines, newspapers, high-interest, low-difficulty novels, illustrated books, photography books, and books with accompanying audiotapes. Encourage students to bring materials if they wish.

Process:

Select material
Read silently
Comment informally

Select material

Take the lead by selecting something to read and settling in. Suggest that students find something to read that interests them.

Read silently

Quietly, you and the students read, listen to tapes with headphones, or look at pictures. If students are not engaged, give a gentle reminder that there are only a few minutes left, or halt the SSR time early.

Comment informally

Students may or may not want to talk after reading. Provide an open atmosphere so students can share a few brief comments or questions. Then, make a clear transition and move on to the next activity.

---

* From *Reading Is Only the Tiger's Tail*, by R. A. McCracken and M. J. McCracken, Lewswing, 1972.

CHAPTER 4   READING DIFFERENT TYPES OF TEXT

One crucial step in becoming a proficient reader is learning that there are different types of text. Each type of text contains specific kinds of information and is meant to be read in its own way.

There are also different kinds of publications, such as newspapers, dictionaries, textbooks, and novels. Each kind of publication has features that distinguish it from all others. Most newspapers are organized in a similar way and have similar types of information. A person who is familiar with *News for You,* an easy-to-read newspaper written especially for adult learners, knows a lot about how to read a difficult paper like the *New York Times.*

By helping students learn the distinguishing features of publications, you help them develop a framework they can use every time they encounter that type of text. They learn how the text is arranged and how they are expected to read it. They become able to use it effectively, the way it was designed to be used.

Just as there are different types of publications, there are also different genres, or types of writing. A story is different from a nonfiction article, and both are different from a letter to the editor in a newspaper.

Learning about different genres or types of writing helps students become aware of type of text as an important dimension of reading and writing. As readers, they learn to use the pattern or structure to build their own version of the text as they read, which helps them understand and remember what they read. They also learn to use the pattern or structure of a type of writing as a guide when they write.

This chapter includes activities for reading different types of publications (newspapers, dictionaries, and textbooks) and for reading different genres (poems, fiction, letters to the editor, and nonfiction).

Discovering Features of a Text

This activity introduces students to the different features of an unfamiliar type of print material or genre. It can be used to introduce students to material, such as a newspaper or dictionary, or to a genre of writing, such as poetry, fiction, news reports, or letters to the editor.

In planning for the activity, take note of important text features. In the activity, you and your students discuss features of the type of text and make a list. Using the list, students search a text for examples of each feature. Then students share what they learned with the group.

The number of features you introduce may vary depending on the level of your students. Basic parts of textbooks are title page, table of contents, chapter titles, and page numbers. Textbooks may also have indexes and appendices. Some basic features of stories are characters, events, a problem, attempts to solve the problem, resolution, and theme. For information and opinion, you could focus on title, headings and subheadings, statements of fact, opinions, and summaries.

Purpose: To introduce students to a new type of text whenever they show an interest or need to use that particular kind of text.

Materials: Copies of one or more texts of the same type, a chalkboard or flip chart, a handout with a list of text features (optional).

Process:

- Lead-in
- Preview
- Whole group search
- Small group search
- Reconvene and report

Lead-in

Remind students of what prompted this activity. It may have been discussion or questions some students had, requests for information commonly found in this kind of text, or GED requirements to understand this type of text.

Preview

Ask students what they already know about features of this type of text. List their answers on the chalkboard or flip chart. If you are not using a handout, put major features that you want to introduce on the list.

Whole group search

To provide initial practice, have the whole group locate one major feature. For example, if you are using a type of text with a table of contents, ask students to locate the table of contents. Then, ask students to use the table of contents to find one other item on the feature list. Once students give the page number for an item, have them find the actual item in the text.

Small group search

Divide into working groups or pairs. Try to form groups that are balanced and have collectively equal reading and problem-solving abilities. Give each group a list of features to locate and a time frame (20 minutes is average, depending on the size of the list). To complete their task, students provide the page number for the example they found, and describe anything new that they learned about the feature from studying the example.

Reconvene and report

When the time is up, have each group report to the whole group on what they found. Ask the groups to add to the list of features. For any item, students can provide a new definition, state its benefits, or provide any other information about the feature that interests them. Let students know that as they use this type of text in the future, they will develop even more strategies for reading this particular type of text.

Sample: Discovering Features of a Text

Finding What's in a Newspaper

Students became familiar with the features of a newspaper so they could find the kinds of information that newspapers provide. The class used a variety of newspapers to accommodate different reading levels. They used *News for You* (New Readers Press) for developing and intermediate readers, the local newspaper for intermediate and advanced readers, and papers like the *New York Times* for advanced readers.

Materials: Copies of newspapers for each working group, a newspaper-hunt handout (see Items for a Newspaper Hunt on page 48), flip chart or chalkboard, markers.

Lead-in

Teacher: After the discussion we had about current events, we decided to start keeping up with the news together. Here are the newspapers I promised to bring.

Preview

Students named sections and types of items found in the newspaper. As the list grew, the teacher suggested some items that the students had not mentioned.

Teacher: What kinds of things would you expect to find in newspapers? I'll write the list on the board.
Students: News. Sports. Pictures.
Teacher: Yes. How about news headlines and captions under the pictures?
Student: Yeah, and comics.

Whole group search

The teacher then led the group through the process of finding a type of item by using the index. When they were successful, they were ready to begin finding things for themselves.

Teacher: Let's see what we can find in this newspaper. First, we'll locate the index on the front page. The index is like the table of contents of a book and can be used to find things in the newspaper. The letter is for the section of the paper and the number is for the page.

Small group search

The class divided into small working groups. The teacher gave each group a newspaper, the newspaper-hunt handout she had prepared, and directions.

Teacher: Use the information on the handout and what you already know about using a newspaper to locate as many items as you can. As you go through the handout answering the questions, you will be discovering things for yourselves and using group problem-solving skills. When you find the item in the paper, circle it with a marker, and record the section and page number on the handout. Then, go on to the next item. Take about 20 minutes.

Reconvene and report

The whole group reconvened. The teacher asked each group to tape newspaper pages to the wall so the group could use them in reporting what they found.

After reporting on the types of items they found, the class discussed what they had discovered about newspapers. They did not have time to complete the whole list.

NOTES ─────────────────────────

Other things we can do:

1) Explore how newspaper articles are organized to answer Who? What? When? Where? How?

2) Talk about the way articles are written so editors can cut from the bottom up to save space.

3) Talk about the purpose of editorials and political cartoons.

4) Explore bias by comparing articles in different newspapers and reading about events students are close to.

Items for a Newspaper Hunt

Directions: Use this list to learn about what is in a newspaper. Write down the section and page number of the items you find.

Item	Section/page	What did you learn about it?
Headline: *large title of an article*		
Subheading: *small title that gives more information*		
Byline: *tells who wrote an article*		
Dateline: *a line telling when and where an article was written*		
Photos and captions: *pictures and the words that explain them*		
Local news: *reports on happenings in the area*		
National news: *reports on happenings in the United States*		
International news: *reports on happenings outside the United States*		
Feature articles: *food, health, and other information people like to read about*		
Editorials: *opinions of the people who run the paper*		
Letters to the editor: *opinions of people who write to the paper*		
Sports: *articles about games, players, and teams*		
Weather: *maps and other information about the weather*		
Obituaries: *announcements of deaths*		
Movies and TV listings: *list of when, where, and what shows are playing*		
Comics: *drawings and words that entertain us*		
Horoscope: *an entertaining way to check on your day*		
Classified ads: *small ads arranged by subject, such as employment, housing, cars, and personals*		
Display ads: *larger ads for merchandise and services*		

Reading Different Types of Text

Sample: Discovering Features of a Text
Finding What's in a Dictionary

Students became familiar with the features of a dictionary so they could use them for vocabulary work. A selection of dictionaries was available to accommodate various reading levels.

Materials: A copy of a dictionary for each small group, flip chart or chalkboard.

Lead-in

Teacher: Today, we can spend some time learning how to use dictionaries so it will be easier for you to look up words.

Preview

Together, the teacher and students listed the kinds of things that people could expect to find in a dictionary. The students named features they already knew and the teacher added other items to the list.

Items in a Dictionary

word	example of use	two guide words on each page
how to spell it	part of speech	a guide to pronunciations
definition	pronunciation	a guide to abbreviations
illustrations	history of word	names or other information

Whole group search

The class used the table of contents in the front of the dictionary to locate the pronunciation guide. They examined the pronunciation marks and looked up several words to see how they were used. Next, the teacher pointed out the two guide words on the top of each page and asked the students to figure out what they were for. Students realized that the guide words helped people identify what words were on the page.

Small group search

The teacher divided the class into groups of four, making sure there was a talker, a leader, and a good reader in each group. She assigned each group a few features to hunt for. Students wrote definitions for their items and what they had learned about them. The teacher visited each group to help them. As some groups completed their list, they were asked to help others.

Reconvene and report

After the class pooled their information, the teacher suggested that in a future activity they could locate words and choose among definitions to create sentences.

Sample: Discovering Features of a Text

Using a Textbook

This type of activity can help students use textbooks and reference material to research a topic. Students who were already familiar with the features of a textbook learned how to use those features to locate specific information.

A group of students in a large GED class at a community college planned to study cosmetology at the college after passing the GED test. They wanted to get some experience with a cosmetology textbook so they would feel more prepared for their next course of study. The teacher borrowed a cosmetology textbook from another instructor.* She helped the students use the features of the textbook to find information that interested them.

Preview

Teacher: What do you already know about reading textbooks?

Students: It's not always best to read a textbook from beginning to end. Sometimes it is smarter to read parts of it or read it in a different order. The way you read a textbook depends on what you want to get from it.

Whole group search

The group reviewed the basic features of a textbook.

Teacher: Find the four things in most textbooks that help people locate information fast. Look for the table of contents, the index, chapter titles and section headings, and summaries.

Next, the group decided what information they wanted from the textbook.

Teacher: What does the book cover?

Student: Makeup and skin care.

Teacher: What do we want to find out first?

Student: How what you eat affects your skin.

Small group search

Teacher: OK. Now that you have decided what you want to find out about, let's use the table of contents and index first. Divide into pairs. In each pair, one person will be A and the other person will be B. The A's look over the table of contents. The B's look in the index. Try to find the chapters or pages that give information on how eating affects your complexion. Write down what you find.

Reconvene and report

Teacher: Let's compare what the people who used the table of contents did with what the people who used the index did.

---

* *Standard Textbook for Professional Estheticians,* by Joel Gerson and Bobbi R. Madry, edited by Israel Rubinstein, Milady, 1986.

Most of the students who had looked at the table of contents reported that the first place they looked was "Part 2: Understanding the Skin and Its Functions." But that didn't produce anything, so they tried "Part 3: Practices and Procedures" and found that chapter 14 was titled "Nutrition and the Health of the Skin." This seemed promising, so they wrote down the page numbers.

One student who had looked in the index reported that she first tried to find the word *food,* but it wasn't listed. Then she tried to look up *chocolate* because that is the food most people associate with skin problems. But it wasn't listed, either. After the teacher suggested that she look for a synonym for food, she thought of *nutrition.* She looked it up and found 10 entries. As she recorded the page numbers, she realized that all the pages dealing with nutrition were close together.

Through this discussion, the students discovered that they had found the same chapter by starting from either the table of contents or the index.

Small group search

Teacher: Now that you know what pages to search, you need to find the specific information. Go to chapter 14. The A's will read the titles and section headings while the B's look at the chapter summary. Make notes on what you find.

Reconvene and report

The students who had read the titles and headings discovered that in this particular textbook there were short phrases in the margins to explain what was in each paragraph. Two students said they hoped this would be the textbook they would use in their cosmetology class because it was so clear and easy to read.

The students who had tried to locate the chapter summary only found a list of questions called "Topics for Discussion and Review." None of the questions related to food. They did find a section toward the end of the chapter about different skin colors and treatments for black skin. A lively discussion ensued, and the group decided to look in the table of contents and index to see if there was more information on skin color.

NOTES

The students worked well, but one pair struggled more than the others and may not remember how to locate information in a textbook. Next time, I'll regroup them, so those two students get partners who can model the process for them. Next time, each pair can work on its own topic and report on it to the whole group.

Reading Poems

Poetry is a valuable type of text to use in reading instruction. Poems provide stimulating reading material in a concise format. A poem can use simple language to convey powerful feelings and ideas that readers at all levels can identify with and respond to. Poems invite adult learners to concentrate on language—to see, hear, and feel the power of language. Like visual art, a poem is an excellent stimulus for discussion and writing.

This is a general activity for reading poems with your students. You can quickly touch on some aspects of a poem and become deeply immersed in others. Spend time on those facets that catch the students' attention.

Purpose: To engage students in reading poems.

Materials: Poems and song lyrics.

Process:

> Introduce poetry reading
>
> Read and reread
>
> Invite response
>
> Discuss the poem as a poem
>
> Ask for evaluation

Introduce poetry reading

During several sessions, read aloud short poems that you enjoy. Share your love, appreciation, and enthusiasm for the poems. Before reading a poem to your students, comment on why you chose it.

> **Teacher:** I found this poem in a magazine and wanted to share it with you. Do you have any favorite poems? Tell me what they are. How about a favorite song? A song is like a poem set to music.

Read and reread

Provide several poems for students to look over and have them select the ones they want to read and discuss. Read one of the selected poems aloud so that both the meaning and the rhythm come through. Then, ask if any students would like to read, too. Allow time for the students to read the poem silently before reading aloud. If a word is misread, supply the correct word quietly to keep the flow of reading smooth. If a student reads word by word or pauses at the end of every line, model fluency by reading the same material. Then students can read aloud again. The goal of rereading is for students to become familiar enough with the poem to read it fluently.

Invite response

Begin the discussion by asking students to share their immediate responses to the words, images, and themes of the poem, and by sharing yours.

> **Teacher:** What do you think of this poem? What strikes you about this poem? What's your favorite line? Do you like the words the poet uses? Which ones? What did you picture in your mind? What is the poem about?

Discuss the poem as a poem

Discuss the literal meaning of the poem first.

> **Teacher:** What is going on in this poem? Where does it take place? Who is speaking? What time of day is it? What season of the year?

Discuss the poet's use of language. Use terms that help you and the students talk about the poem. Most students are already familiar with the words *rhythm* and *beat*. Some other terms are:

Imagery: painting a picture with words

Metaphor: comparing or connecting two things not normally associated with each other

Alliteration: repeating beginning sounds

Personification: giving human qualities to things

> **Teacher:** Since poems are usually short, a poet has to choose words very carefully. Let's look at how this poet uses the same words over and over. How does that make you feel? Do the words paint a picture for you?

Look at any unusual features of layout, punctuation, capitalization, word usage, or dialect used in the poem for the ways they convey meaning. Discuss the effects they produce.

> **Teacher:** Look at the way the poet capitalizes certain words every time they appear in the poem. Why do you think he does that? The first and last lines are exactly the same. What do you make of that? This poet uses *ain't* and *gonna* and *askin*. Why does he do that?

Interpret the poem together. Explore students' responses to the poem on a broader level. Through these many turns with the poem, students' opinions and responses will probably have become more focused and detailed. Ask students for their responses again.

> **Teacher:** Now that we've talked about what happens in the poem and the way the poet uses language, what do you think the poem is really about? What ideas or attitudes come across in this poem? What ideas do you get from reading the poem? What do you think about this poem? Would you like to create a poem yourself?

Ask for evaluation

Encourage students to capture their experience of reading poems. Suggest that they write a poem, or write about how they feel when they read poems, or write about what poems do.

Note: Adult learners may come to poetry with many preconceived ideas. Some adult learners consider reading poetry a frivolous pastime. They may say, "This stuff is OK, but I came here to learn to read. I need to be working in a workbook." Explain that many reading and writing skills can be developed by reading, writing, and discussing poetry. Point out that writing poetry is a good way for people to express what they experience.

Another preconceived idea many students have is that every line has to "mean" something, which they in turn must clearly understand. They may read a poem and get frustrated thinking they don't "get it," rather than allowing themselves the opportunity to savor the language and respond to the sensations they experience.

Sometimes, adults expect that each question asked about a poem has one right answer. This is not the case. As with other art forms, personal experiences and background knowledge combine with the words on the page to produce different interpretations for different readers. When you ask questions dealing with interpretation, you might say, "There are no right or wrong answers here. Your understanding of a poem will depend on the poem plus your own experiences."

Sample: Reading Poems

Exploring a Poem

A teacher introduced her student to short, easy-to-read poems. Reading poems helped the student improve her fluency in reading and increased her ability to read for meaning. In this activity, the student selected a poem she liked and explored the poem with her teacher in two 30-minute activities across two sessions.

Introduce poetry reading

Teacher: Janet, I brought something new for you to read. I thought you might enjoy reading some poems.

Read and reread

The teacher brought in a collection of easy-to-read poems and chose several short poems to read aloud with the student. As the teacher read, she encouraged the student to read along whenever she felt like it. Then the teacher asked the student to choose a poem to read first silently, and then aloud. When she misread a word, the teacher supplied it, quietly.

This is the poem Janet chose to read.

> Red
>
> Red houses,
> Red barns
> And red berries
> Are nice
> For gray and brown winters.
> They are spice
> On plain land
> Till snow and sky plan
> Something new.
> And winter is red, white and blue.

From *Sky Bridges and Other Poems*, by Ruth Yaffe Radin, New Readers Press, 1993.

Student: Red horses		**Teacher:** Houses	
Student: They are . . .		**Teacher:** Spice	
Student: On plan		**Teacher:** Plain	

In the first reading, the student did not read with the ease needed to understand the sense of the poem or appreciate its images or language. So the teacher modeled reading.

Teacher: I like that poem. Now, let me read it to you.

The teacher read the poem.

Teacher: How does it sound?
Student: Pretty.

Teacher: We can read this poem in sentences to get the sense of it. Here's the first sentence: "Red houses / Red barns / And red berries / Are nice / For gray and brown winters." Now, you read the sentence.

The teacher and student took turns reading the sentences of the poem. Then the student read the poem again by herself. This time she read fluently.

Invite response

Teacher: Did you like that poem? What did you like about it?

Student: I like all those pretty colors. It's just like outside. And then at the end, it reminded me of the flag—red, white, and blue. I'd like to write like that.

Discuss the poem as a poem

Teacher: What do you think this poem is talking about?

Student: It talks about the barn.

Teacher: Can you see a barn when you shut your eyes?

Student: Yeah. A red one.

Teacher: This poem's imagery is created with colors. What colors are in it?

Student: Red, red, red, gray, red, white, and blue. That's why I like it.

Teacher: Great. Look at the lines of the poems. What do you see?

Student: They've got colors in them. And the title is "Red."

Teacher: Those colors must be important for us to read. Why do you think the poet uses those particular colors?

Student: She probably likes to paint.

Teacher: Do you see that the red house, barns, and berries are like something else?

Student: Well, your blood is red and valentines are red.

Teacher: That's right. And the red things are compared to spice. See?

(She points to the lines and reads, "They are spice / On plain land.")

Student: Because the grass is dead.

Teacher: The grass is dead, so there's no color . . .

Student: Except that red. It's like ketchup on meat loaf.

Teacher: Exactly!

At the end of the activity, the student said that she wanted to read more poems. The teacher remembered that she had also wanted to write one.

Sample: Reading Poems

Writing a Poem after Reading a Poem

In this activity, the student wrote her first poem with the teacher's assistance. The teacher made an outline patterned on the poem that the student had read. She used the language experience approach to write down the student's first draft. The student copied and revised the poem at home and brought it to their next session to read and enjoy.

Process:

> Choose a topic

> Write and read a first draft

> Revise and read the poem

Choose a topic

Teacher: You said before that you wanted to write a poem. Are you still interested?
Student: I liked the poem "Red." I want to write a poem like that.
Teacher: We can use it as a guide. What would you like to use from it?
Student: I want to write about colors. Like in the poem.
Teacher: What's your favorite color?
Student: White.

Write and read a first draft

Teacher: What if we use "Red" as a model?

The teacher jotted down the following outline. As the student talked, the teacher wrote the words.

> White _____
> White _____
> White _____
> White _____

Teacher: Now, which words would you like to use to fill in the blanks?
Student: White snow, white rugs, white flowers, and white tile. Dresser drawers is white and light is white, too.
Teacher: Anything else?
Student: No.
Teacher: OK. Now you could say why you like white.
Student: I like it because it looks clean and brand new. And sometimes it sparkles.

The teacher wrote, "White looks clean and brand new. Sometimes it sparkles."

Teacher: Do you want a title for your poem?

Student: "White." Just like "Red."
Teacher: Now I want you to read what I wrote down.
Student: I can't read all that.
Teacher: Well, you said all that. These are your words.

The student read, misreading a few words, which the teacher corrected.

Janet's poem, first draft
White
White snow
White rugs
White flowers
And white tile.
Dresser drawers is white.
And light is white, too.
White looks clean and brand new.
Sometimes it sparkles.

Revise and read the poem

Teacher: This is the rough draft of your poem, Janet. Take it home and reread it. Figure out what you want to put in the final draft.
Student: Don't I have to use what's here?
Teacher: It's your poem. You can use whatever you think sounds good.
Student: I want the words to sound pretty.

The student worked on her poem at home, rereading it and trying out changes. Then she copied her revised poem. In the next session, she read her poem to the teacher. She read more fluently.

Teacher: Are you satisfied with the poem the way it is now?
Student: Yes, I like it.

Janet's Poem

White
White snow
White rugs
White flowers
And white tile
Look brand new.
Light is white.
I like white.

Reprinted by permission of the author, Janet P. Evans.

Reading Fiction

Stories, especially folktales and other traditional stories, have a well-defined structure with specific parts. Knowing the parts of the story can help students recognize and remember the plot and theme when they read. In this activity, the teacher introduces students to key elements of a story. The class reads the story and fills out the key elements for the story they read.

You can chart the parts of a story on a chalkboard or hand out a chart to the students to complete. (See the Fiction Chart on page 61.)

Purpose: To help students use main elements of a story to understand and remember stories they read.

Materials: A story or narrative poem, chalkboard or fiction chart.

Process:
> Preview
>
> Introduce story elements
>
> Read and chart
>
> Discuss

Preview

Discuss what students already know about fiction. What is fiction? What elements do we usually find in a piece of fiction? Help students understand that while fiction is made up from the author's imagination, it can often help us to understand our own lives more clearly.

Introduce story elements

List the elements of a story or hand out a fiction chart. Briefly explain each element of the chart and how to use it.

> **Teacher:** Each element on the fiction chart can be found in most stories. They are things to notice as you read. Look for character clues. What is the main character like? Look for the character's reactions to main events in the story. How does the main character feel or react to what's happened? Look for the main problems or conflicts in the story. How does the main character attempt to solve the problems? Is the character successful? How are the problems solved?

Authors tell stories for a reason. After you have read the story, think about the author's message or theme. What is the author's point in telling the story?

Read and chart

Teacher modeling. To show students how to look for story elements, read a short story together and model how you locate information for each element. Think aloud so students can hear your reasoning as you decide which information fits each element. If you can't decide which information fits, say so.

Whole group charting. During the next session, read another story. Ask students to say what fits each element. Allow them to discuss possible answers. Let them disagree with each other if necessary, and then try to come to a consensus.

Small group charting. During the next session, read a third story and ask students to work in groups to locate information. You can circulate among the groups to make sure they understand the task, and to give support.

Independent charting. Ask students to list information for each element when they read fiction. Phase out this practice when they have learned to think about the elements of a story on their own.

Discuss

When students discuss their responses, make sure that all ideas are entertained and that no one is told they are wrong. If students give an unexpected response, let them defend their ideas with information from the text or from their personal experience.

Students may be able to follow the story line (plot) and discuss it sooner than they are able to talk about the theme. It may take several discussions on what a theme is before students begin to abstract the theme from the story. Often stories have more than one theme. It is not necessary to agree on a single theme.

Fiction Chart

Name _____ Date _____

Story Title and Author _____

Main Character _____

Character Clues: What is the main character like?

Reactions: How does the main character react or feel about important events in the story?

Problems: List the problems or conflicts. Circle the main problem.

Attempts: How do the characters try to solve the problems?

Resolutions: How does the main problem get solved, or is it left unsolved?

Theme: What is the author's message?

Sample: Reading Fiction
Charting a Story

When students in a mixed-level class asked for a definition of fiction, the teacher introduced the class to key elements of a story. She selected an easy-to-read story so all of the students could participate in charting and discussing its parts.

Materials: A myth adapted for new readers.

Preview

When asked what they already knew about fiction, some students said that fiction was not true. The teacher suggested that authors use their own experiences to enrich their writing. Some stories are true; some are not. The class talked about movies and TV shows that were like real life even though the characters that the actors portray are not actual living people. Eventually the group agreed that fiction is made-up stories that often help us understand more about ourselves and our lives.

Read and chart

The teacher handed out a fiction chart and explained each element. Then each student turned to the story "Pandora's Box" in *Myths*. The teacher read aloud as students followed along. Then the class filled out the chart together.

Teacher: Who is the main character?
Student: Pandora.
Teacher: What do you know about her from reading the story?
Student: She is the goddess of love.
Teacher: Show me where in the text that idea appears or what in your experience tells you that.
Student: I read it. It says . . . Oh, it's Aphrodite. I mixed her up with Pandora.

The students clarified their interpretations and reached consensus on most items. One student said that Pandora started as a statue. He explained that he thought this because Zeus made her out of clay. Other students agreed that he could be right. Coming to consensus, the group filled in the rest of the chart. They had difficulty deciding on Pandora's reaction to the escape of evil into the world. Finally, they just noted that the story did not say how she felt.

Discuss

Talking about the theme touched off a debate. Some men said that the moral of the story was that women should listen to men. Women responded that the story showed how brave women are and how cowardly men can be. They discussed the story of Adam and Eve and the differences between religion and myth. No consensus was reached, but the class engaged in a lively discussion.

Pandora's Box

At one time, there were men on earth but no women. Zeus asked for the gods' help in making the first woman. The son of Zeus took some clay and gave the woman a shape.

The Four Winds blew life into her. Aphrodite (AFF-row-DIE-tee), the goddess of love and beauty, gave the woman soft skin and a pretty smell and filled her with love. Athena (uh-THEEN-uh), the goddess of wisdom, gave the woman a strong mind. Hera (HAIR-uh), the queen of the gods, made her curious. The woman would always want to know about things.

The first woman had everything. The gods named her Pandora (pan-DOOR-uh). This means "the gift of all." Then they gave her to a mortal named Epimetheus (EPP-uh-MEE-thee-us), to be his wife. Along with Pandora came a box. It was a gift to her new husband from the gods. They did not tell Pandora what was inside.

Epimetheus and Pandora fell very much in love. "Why should I be so lucky?" Epimetheus wondered. "Why should the gods give me such a perfect woman?"

"Please don't ask such questions," said Pandora. "Just open the box. I want to see my gift to you."

"No," said Epimetheus. "I don't trust the gods. We must never open the box. It may be a trick."

So the box stayed closed.

But Pandora grew more and more curious as to what was inside it. One day Epimetheus was away. "I must see what is in the box," Pandora said to herself. "I will only look inside. I will not touch a thing."

She slowly lifted the lid of the box. Out flew all sorts of ugly monsters. Sickness, Sadness, and Hate flew out of the box and into the world. Pandora banged down the lid as fast as she could. But all the bad things were already loose. Now the world would just have to live with them.

When Epimetheus got home, Pandora told him what she had done. He was very sad to hear the news. He went over to the box. "Listen!" He said. "I hear a noise. Something else is still in there. Go ahead and lift the lid again. Surely, nothing could be worse than what already flew out."

Pandora lifted the lid. There, at the bottom, was Hope. It, too, flew out of the box and into the world.

This was just what the world needed. The people would have many bad things to deal with. But now, no matter what happened, there would always be Hope.

From *Myths,* by Tana Reiff, New Readers Press, 1991.

Fiction Chart

Name __Reading Group__   Date __April 12__

Story Title and Author __Pandora's Box__

Main Character __Pandora__

Character Clues: What is the main character like?

curious	1st female	started as a statue
pretty	strong-minded	pretty smell
concerned	soft skin	filled with love

Reactions: How does the main character react or feel about important events in the story?

He felt sad that Pandora had opened the box; but it doesn't say how she felt.

Problems: List the problems or conflicts. Circle the main problem.

Gods trying to trick us.	She was nervous about opening the box.
She didn't listen to her man.	She wanted to open the box.
Man blamed her.	(She let bad things out into the world.)

Attempts: How do the characters try to solve the problems?

At first, she didn't open the box. Then, later, she opened the box.

Resolutions: How does the main problem get solved, or is it left unsolved?

Live with the bad things. (Trust in God.)
Let the bad things out but Hope got out, too. That was good.
Good balanced the bad in the end. She took a risk, a chance.

Theme: What is the author's message?

Hope is only a "could be."	There are rainy days but also sunny ones.
Listen to your man!	Women are strong. Men are cowards.
Hope turns the world around.	Are women the source of evil (Adam and Eve)?

Reading Different Types of Text   61

Reading Letters to the Editor

Letters to the editor, like editorials, are types of writing that are similar to an essay. In this activity you can introduce students to key features of a letter to the editor as a way to communicate on public issues.

Purpose: To help students become familiar with letters to the editor.

Material: Copies of two letters to the editor on the same subject, a flip chart or chalkboard.

Process:

Preread and read

Brainstorm features

Identify features

Prepare for writing

Preread and read

Distribute a pair of letters to the editor on one subject. Briefly discuss what letters to the editors are, so students can recall what they already know about them. Then, ask students to read both letters or to follow along as you read them aloud. As they read, have them look for features that make up a letter to the editor.

Brainstorm features

Ask students to brainstorm a list of features they found in both letters. You may point out such things as a strong opinion clearly stated, supporting reasons for the author's belief, facts from the author's point of view, a title, and the author's name.

Identify features

Together, students locate the features in the letters. Help students discuss what they did and how they decided that they had found the specific feature.

Prepare for writing

Ask students to write a brief note about what they found and learned. Give them about two minutes to write. Read the notes to see if students understand letters to the editor. If they do, they can write their own letters about an issue they have been studying.

Sample: Reading Letters to the Editor

Reading to Write Letters to the Editor

Students living in a housing project wanted to write letters to the editor to voice their dissatisfaction with the way the authorities had handled a recent crime wave. To help them learn features of a letter to the editor, the teacher brought in copies of two letters to the editor that presented different views on the same subject. After listing key features, students marked the letters to highlight each type of information they had identified.

Purpose: To help students identify important types of information in a letter to the editor so they could write their own.

Materials: Copies of two letters to the editor, sets of markers, chalkboard or flip chart.

Preread and read

Teacher: What do you already know about letters to the editor?
Student: They are letters printed in the newspaper.

The teacher paired less experienced readers with stronger readers and asked them to read the letters together. After reading, the whole class briefly discussed content to make sure everyone had understood the letters.

Teacher: What is the issue in these letters, and what do the authors think?
Students: The two letters disagree. One writer is a smoker and the other isn't. The first letter writer is angry that the government isn't doing enough and is worried that lawmakers might be getting bribed.

Then the teacher suggested that they read the letters again, this time looking for what makes up a letter to the editor. The teacher read aloud and asked the students to read along.

Letters to the Editor

Lawmakers unconcerned about hazards of tobacco

The recent furor over E. coli contamination of hamburger highlights the contrast between the action the government is capable of taking when the public interest is not in conflict with the self-interest of our lawmakers and when the reverse is true.

Although cigarettes are a $26 billion business and the leading cause of death from cancer, heart disease and other disorders, and the government has mandated warning labels on all cigarette packages and advertising, our legislators are not sufficiently concerned with the nation's health to remove the subsidy on tobacco.

Could it be that there is a conflict between the self-interests of the president and Congress and any attempt to persuade the tobacco barons to convert to other beneficial crops? Surely the hazard of E. coli in hamburger is not greater than the hazard of cigarette smoking.

Equally strange is the lack of any significant outcry about the tobacco hazard from the media, who are quick to jump on some obscure problem. Could the question of self-interest also deter them from voicing their collective outrage at this anomaly? Isn't anybody asking why?

Daniel A. Lundy, Bellevue

Another nitwit idea

I can't believe some of the muddled people in Olympia. Imagine—more invasion of our privacy by outlawing smoking in our private autos.

What next? The Gestapo invading our homes to see if we smoke, eat beef or use colored toilet paper?

My response to their nitwit ideas is "Up your cigarette butts."

Elizabeth J. Lysne, Tacoma

From the *Seattle Times*, Feb. 26, 1993. Reprinted by permission of the publisher.

Brainstorm features

Students listed the features they found. The teacher prompted further discussion and rereading of some parts of the letters to help the students add supporting reasons and facts to the list.

Identify features

Teacher: Now, go back to the letters. Identify each of the features we listed. Here is a set of markers for each pair. Use them to highlight the title in green, facts in blue, questions in yellow, and positions in pink.

Features of a
letter to the editor

title	questions
name at the end	opinion (a position)
the town where the person lives	supporting reasons
facts	

As the group identified examples of each feature in both letters, students described strategies they had used to find them. One student said she looked for different supporting reasons in each paragraph.

> **Teacher:** Oh, you used what you already knew about good paragraphs—that they concentrate on explaining one idea.

The group discussed opinions versus facts, and how to use reasons to convince someone. One student commented that it's not a good idea always to agree on everything. Some things need to be argued about.

Prepare for writing

The group discussed ideas for their own letters.

Reading Nonfiction: Taking Note of Information

Whether reading a magazine for pleasure or studying a textbook, students need a strategy to gain information from nonfiction reading material. In this activity, students learn a strategy of noting important points as they read and making comments about them by using "double-entry note taking." Students draw two columns on a piece of paper. As they read, they note and write down important points of information in column one. Then they write a personal association or opinion for each point in column two.

Purpose: To help students understand and remember information they read.

Materials: A short, interesting nonfiction reading selection.

Process:

> Introduce the strategy

> Read and take notes

> Share and respond (optional)

Introduce the strategy

Introduce the double-entry note-taking strategy. Show students how to take notes on important or interesting points they read. Then, show them how to write comments on each point. Provide each student with a copy of a short nonfiction reading selection. Ask students to fold a sheet of paper in two and label each half.

Read and take notes

Read the selection with the students. Then, model the strategy. Start with the "What I read" column. Pick out facts, quotes, or summaries. Write brief notes. Say aloud your reasoning for including each point. Then, invite students to suggest points. Next, fill out the "What I think" column. If you disagree with or question the text, make sure the students see that in action. Talk through a section or point you disagree with. Also, demonstrate how you marvel at new information or praise the text's defense of an idea you agree with. Invite students to comment on their points. Then, have students read on their own and take notes. Later, they can use their notes to write about what they read.

Share and respond (optional)

By adding a third column labeled "Responses by others," students can share their notes and write responses to each others' entries.

Sample: Reading Nonfiction: Taking Note of Information
Doing Double-Entry Note Taking

Students wanted help remembering what they read in a science article on rain forests.

Introduce the strategy

> **Teacher:** Double-entry note taking is a strategy to help you notice and remember what you read.

Read and take notes

The teacher handed out a reading selection she had adapted and shortened. She drew two columns on the chalkboard: "What I read" and "What I think."

At first the teacher provided some items. Then she invited the students to contribute. The group completed the "What I read" column first. Then they made comments in the "What I think" column.

In modeling how to fill out the "What I read" column, the teacher summarized a fact from the first paragraph of the reading selection. For the second paragraph, she wrote down something that interested her.

> **Teacher:** I didn't write down what I thought was the author's most important idea in that paragraph. Instead, I wrote down information that interested me.

For the third paragraph, she again summarized a main idea. For the next paragraph, she invited suggestions from the students.

> **Student:** Put in "forest floor is bare."
> **Teacher:** What should I put in for the fifth paragraph?
> **Students:** Soil is not fertile. Bugs are nutritious.
> **Teacher:** OK, but explain to me what fertile means.

They talked briefly about erosion and the fertility of the rain forests. For the last paragraph they discussed how giant snails are interesting, but decided they wanted to note the main idea instead.

For the "What I think" column, the teacher modeled her opinions and associations for the items in the first three paragraphs and then invited students to provide the remaining entries.

> **Teacher:** Why did you select "forest floor is bare"?
> **Student:** That's so different from our forests.

Then the students put aside the reading selection and wrote everything they remembered about what they had read, using their notes if they wanted.

What about Rain Forests?

Rain forests have layers of plants and animals. The highest plant layer, or tree canopy, is between 100 and 165 feet above the ground. It is so dense that it keeps most of the light and lots of the water from reaching the ground. Most of the food for the animals is found among the leaves and branches of the canopy, where a lot of the animals live, swinging, gliding, and leaping to find food and escape predators. The animals—monkeys, flying squirrels, sharp-clawed woodpeckers, and thousands of others—rarely need to come down to the ground level at all.

The next layer down in the rain forest is filled with small trees, climbing plants, orchids, fruits, nuts, and ferns. Some of these are parasitic, meaning they steal life from the larger trees. Other plants just use the bigger trees for support.

The space just above the ground surface is occupied by tree branches, twigs, and leaves. Many kinds of animals run, hop, flutter, and climb in the undergrowth. Most of these animals live on insects and fruit, although a few are meat eaters. They tend to communicate more by sound than by sight in this dense, dark layer.

Most of the forest floor is bare, except for a thin layer of humus and fallen leaves. The animals inhabiting this ground layer—like rhinoceroses, chimpanzees, gorillas, elephants, deer, leopards, and bears—have adapted to walking and climbing short distances.

Below the soil surface, burrowing creatures, such as armadillos, bugs, and microorganisms work to decompose the organic litter that falls from above. Most rain forest soils tend to be permanently moist and soggy. Although these soils are rich in certain minerals, most of the minerals are washed out of the soil by water passing over it.

Surprisingly enough, the soils are not very fertile. Most of the nutrition available in the rain forest is stored in plants, animals, and microorganisms, not in the soil. When leaves or trees fall or animals die, they are quickly decomposed by various organisms like beetles, fungi, and bacteria. The bodies of these small beings or the waste they produce provide nutrition for the rest of the forest.

There is an enormous number of different animals present in rain forests, and their variety is astounding. Some can be gigantic, such as huge snails and butterflies. Some are quick; others have camouflage to hide them, and others are nocturnal feeders in order to escape predators.

Adapted from Global Tomorrow Coalition (Walter H. Corson, editor) *The Global Ecology Handbook: What You Can Do About the Environmental Crisis,* Beacon Press, 1990. Adapted and printed by permission of the publisher.

Double-Entry Notes

What I read	What I think
highest layer is canopy, hard for light and water to get through things	dark, wet and full of living . . . ugh
Parasitic is stealing life from others	like fleas only really big, ugh again
	interesting idea
Undergrowth layer—dark, lots of animals communicate with sound	like bats???
Forest floor is bare	Not like our forests!
soil not fertile/bugs are nutritious	I'd starve first!
big variety of animals	more than we have? Sounds like it

CHAPTER 5 TEACHABLE MOMENTS IN READING

As teachers, we have all experienced those brief and valued moments when the lines of communication between teacher and learner open wide. These "teachable moments" grace instruction unexpectedly and fleetingly. They are spontaneous occasions for on-the-spot teaching and learning that bring together the learner's needs and interests with your own resourcefulness.

You can be alert for these times, noticing when the student looks puzzled, is struggling, or asks for help. You can intervene and refocus the situation, changing a difficulty into a learning opportunity. These times are also opportunities for drawing attention to things the student has done well. Celebrating achievements helps students become aware of what they know so they can gain further control over it.

Every aspect of instruction can be furthered during teachable moments. Teachable moments are times when you can help a learner apply what has been previously taught as well as introduce new areas of instruction. It is useful to keep notes of what you teach in teachable moments, both to track instruction and to refer to in planning future lessons.

Capitalizing on teachable moments requires a willingness to change direction, but only with the learner's full permission and involvement. It means recognizing the moment and making a conscious decision to alter instruction to capitalize on it. It means allowing lessons to be carried in new directions and sometimes leaving behind the most carefully planned lessons in favor of a sense of discovery. It means knowing that the unexpected can have important educational results for you and your students.

The examples in this chapter show how teachable moments are used to help students gain skill in recognizing words, catching a miscue, exploring punctuation, reading for meaning, and using phonics for decoding and blending.

Using Context to Recognize Words

A teacher helps a student use context to check for word meaning.

During a reading-instruction activity, a student is having trouble understanding parts of a selection even though she is familiar with the subject and understands the general message. The teacher asks the student to read aloud and notices that she misreads several words. The student seems to be relying on phonics clues but is not using context to recognize words.

> . . . it takes longer to train a cat as a pet than it does to train a dog
>
> The United States has more cats than any other country. It has been recorded that more than twenty-eight million cats live in the United States.
>
> People who love cats can do strange things sometimes. A doctor on the . . .

From "Cats," in *Challenger 2 Adult Reading Series*, by Corea Murphy, New Readers Press, 1985.

Student: (Reading) "The United States has more cats than any other county. It has been recruited that more than twenty-eight million cats live in the United States."

The Intervention

Teacher: Let's stop for just a minute. What do you think about the way you're reading this selection?

Student: Not much. It's really hard. There are a lot of words I don't know, and I can't seem to sound them out.

Teacher: Yes, I'm noticing that too. But you seem to know what the selection is about. Do you know a lot about cats?

Student: I have two cats and I like them a lot.

Teacher: That seems to be helping you comprehend. We need to work a bit on helping you say the words correctly. Sometimes there are clues you can use. Shall I show you how to use these clues?

Student: Sure, anything that'll help.

Teacher: When you come across a word you don't know or can't pronounce, you can try to figure it out by using the other words around it. For instance, in the sentence, "The United States has more cats than any other country," you read "county." Is the United States a county?

Student: No, it's a country. I should have said "country."

Teacher: Remember that you're trying to make sense when you read. In that sentence the word *country* refers to the United States, so you have a clue to the word. Sometimes you have to look a little farther in the reading, like in this sentence: "It has been recorded that more than twenty-eight million cats live in the United States." You read "recruited."

Student: I did? Well, that was a silly mistake.

Teacher: The trick in this sentence is to look past the word to find clues. The sentence begins with, "It has been ——— that . . ." Usually that kind of sentence construction indicates that something has happened. *Recruited* couldn't fit because the rest of the sentence talks about how many cats live in the United States. Now you know you need a word that fits with that information. The word could be *recorded,* or even *reported,* but *recruited* doesn't fit the meaning.

Student: I see. I guess I don't pay enough attention to the meaning of words when I read, do I?

Teacher: You can learn to. Trying to figure out words by looking for clues in the rest of the sentence is called "using context." As you come to words you don't know in the rest of the selection, let me know and we'll practice using context.

NOTES ————

Lorna missed some pretty obvious context clues today. We talked about her miscues, and I showed her how to use context to identify words. I'll have to plan some lessons on use of context to help her learn this skill.

Catching a Miscue

Making an occasional miscue—misreading a word, punctuation mark, or intonation—is part of reading. Some miscues can be overlooked because they do not alter the meaning of the text. When a miscue does alter meaning, it should be corrected. By pointing out to the student what he has done when he self-corrects a miscue, the teacher helps the student develop an important reading strategy: detecting miscues by checking for meaning.

The Moment

While reading aloud, a student inserts the word *not* and changes the meaning of the sentence. He realizes that the sentence does not make sense. The teacher notices that the student has taken the first step in detecting the miscue. By helping him complete the strategy, and talking about what he has done right this time, the teacher helps him gain awareness, so he can call on the same actions the next time he has trouble making sense of what he reads.

> "If you do get fired, let me know," said Eddie.
>
> "Mike is going to the park with me at ten o'clock. You can go with us if you do get fired."
>
> Mr. Jones did fire Bob, so Bob rode to the park with Eddie and Mike.

From "Bob is Late," in Book 1 of the *Challenger* Adult Reading Series, by Corea Murphy, New Readers Press, 1985.

Student: (Reading) "Mr. Jones did not fire Bob, so Bob rode to the park with Eddie and Mike." Wait a minute. If Mr. Jones didn't fire him, how can Bob go to the park?

The Intervention

The teacher praises the student and draws him back to the sentence to help him discover his misreading.

Teacher: You're being very observant. Did Bob get fired or not? Find the sentence that tells you so and read it again.

Student: "Mr. Jones did fire Bob, so . . ." Oh, he *did* fire him.

Teacher: Right. That's great. You noticed immediately that something was wrong with the meaning, and then you read again to see what went wrong. And you found out what it was, one little word. But those little words are important. How different is that sentence with or without the word *not?*

Student: He either has a job or he doesn't. It's a big difference.

Teacher: You bet. It's good to look for those little words when you read and all of a sudden it stops making sense.

Exploring Punctuation

Using punctuation appropriately is a skill that develops over time. A good way to introduce a punctuation mark is when a student becomes curious about it for the first time.

The Moment

In previous instruction the student has learned about periods, question marks, and commas. But the teacher has not yet pointed out apostrophes and quotation marks. These are more complex, involving direct and indirect speech, contractions, and possessives. Now the student notices the apostrophes and quotation marks and asks his teacher about them.

Student: What are all the comma things? And why are there two of them?

The Intervention

The teacher takes the opportunity provided by the student's question and briefly explains apostrophes and quotation marks.

Teacher: The single marks are called apostrophes. The double ones are called quotation marks. Quotation marks show us the words that someone is saying.

Student: Why don't they just say he's talking? You know, like "he said."

Teacher: That happens sometimes. But sometimes you just see the words he's actually saying. You need the quotation marks to know when he begins to speak and when he stops.

Student: Well, what's this comma thing? Apos . . . what'd you call it?

Teacher: Apostrophe. In the word *didn't,* it means some letters were left out. It really means *did not.* I'll write it out for you.

Sometimes we leave out letters to make our writing sound more like speaking. Then we use an apostrophe to show that something's left out. You can use apostrophes when you write.

Student: Well, I don't know. I want all the letters in when I write.

Teacher: That's OK too. You can choose to write either way. This author chose to use apostrophes. Now you know what they're for.

NOTES ————————

Lonnie asked me about quotation
marks and apostrophes. I gave a
brief explanation. We'll deal with
this again in the future, maybe in
a writing activity.

Using Repeated Reading

A teacher helps a student use a repeated-reading strategy with difficult text.

The Moment

A student has brought in a notice from her daughter's teacher. She is discouraged because she cannot read it. Many words are difficult for her and impair her ability to understand the message.

> **SCHOOL CARNIVAL**
>
> It's time for our annual SCHOOL CARNIVAL here at Grand View School.
>
> The CARNIVAL will be held Saturday, March 19, 1994, in the school cafeteria.
>
> Each class will sponsor their own activity. There will be games and prizes.
>
> Parents are asked to contribute either money or time to the SCHOOL CARNIVAL.
>
> Everyone's participation is needed for our CARNIVAL to be a success.
>
> Proceeds from the CARNIVAL will be used to purchase computers for classrooms.
>
> Our goal is to have a computer in each classroom in the school. It's important to make this CARNIVAL a big success so that we can purchase computers. Please do your part.

The Intervention

The teacher puts aside his planned reading-instruction activity, and shows the student how to use a repeated-reading strategy.

First, the teacher helps her preview the text. He gives the student an opportunity to ask for help with difficult words.

Teacher: Before we try to read the notice, let's get some ideas about what it might say. The title is "School Carnival." Does this suggest what the notice is about?

Student: Well, a carnival is like a circus. It's fun and there are games and things. I guess that means the school is going to have a carnival.

Teacher: Yes, I think that's it. Look at the notice. Do you see any words that you'd like me to read to you?

Student: Let's see. Here, what's this word?

Teacher: "Contribute." Do you know what it means?

Student: *Contribute.* Yes, I've heard it; but I don't think I've ever read that word before. I'll bet they want me to give some money or something.

Teacher: That's exactly right. It says that each parent is asked to contribute money or time to the carnival. Now that we've looked it over, try to read the notice aloud.

The student reads the notice aloud, misses many words, but makes it through the entire piece.

Teacher: Tell me what you just read.

Student: Well, I read that there's going to be a school carnival in March, and that all the classes will do something. I didn't understand this part here. Does it mean they're going to buy computers?

Teacher: Something like that. It means they hope to raise enough money to buy a computer for each classroom. Basically you've got a pretty good idea of the notice. How about reading it again?

The student reads aloud again, this time with fewer mistakes.

Student: Hey, that was easier than the first time I read it. And it made more sense, too.

Teacher: Good. You read it much more fluently. This word still gives you trouble. Can you read it to me and tell me what it means?

Student: "Participation." It means doing something. They want everybody to do something for the carnival.

Teacher: Great. Now, read it once more. This time, I think you'll really surprise yourself.

The student reads aloud for the third time.

Student: Hey, I did it! It was much easier this time.

As they conclude, the teacher reviews what they did. He explains what the repeated-reading strategy is and how to use it.

Teacher: Each time you read the notice, you knew more about what you were reading. Anytime you find yourself trying to read difficult material, you can do what we've done today. Think about what you're going to read, look it over to get some idea of what it's about, and get someone to help you with difficult words. Then, read the passage several times until it makes sense to you.

NOTES

Put aside planned lesson today. Angie brought in a notice from her daughter's school. I'm glad she did. Communication with the school is hard for her. I've encouraged her to bring in things she needs to read. We used repeated reading. It took awhile, but Angie now understands about the school carnival next month, and I think she understands the repeated-reading strategy. We'll try it again soon.

Modeling How to Read for Meaning

A student can learn a lot quickly by observing what an experienced reader does. To help a student read for meaning, the teacher shows him the kinds of thinking she does as she reads.

The Moment

Like many new readers, this student's concern with decoding prevented him from consciously trying to understand what he read. The student read two paragraphs of the article below aloud with excellent word recognition. But he could not tell the teacher the meaning of what he had read. The teacher decided to model her own reading process to help the student develop a strategy of mixing thinking with reading.

> **Sleeping**
>
> On most nights, as you start to get sleepy, you may yawn a few times. Yawning is a very common way in which your body tries to draw in more air.

Teacher: What does the first paragraph tell you about why you yawn?
Student: I don't know.
Teacher: Keep on reading. You'll be able to get the meaning better when you have more information. Read the second paragraph, and look for things that happen as you go to sleep.

> After you go to bed, changes start to happen in your body even before you fall asleep. Your body heat goes down, and your brain waves become more even. When you do fall asleep, your heart rate slows down, your body relaxes, and your breathing becomes very even.

Student: It said something about falling asleep, but I can't remember it.

The Intervention

The teacher steps in to model her own comprehension processes, hoping the student will see how important it is to think while reading. She reviews the two paragraphs that the student has read, repeating the main points and commenting to make personal connections with the information. Then she thinks about what she will find in the third paragraph. She reads the third and fourth paragraphs aloud, commenting on each and drawing the student into thinking about the ideas. Then she asks the student to read the fifth paragraph. The student is able to maintain the active reading that the teacher demonstrated.

Teacher: I'd like to break in here and take a turn reading to you. I'll stop now and then to tell you what I'm thinking.

Let's see. You've already read that yawning is a common way for the body to try to get more air. That's true for me. And I know that as soon as I go to bed I start to relax and breathe evenly. Now, my guess is that the rest of the selection will be about what happens after I'm asleep. I think there'll be something about dreaming. I dream sometimes, but mostly I just sleep. I wake up, and I haven't moved all night.

> Doctors say that we move through four stages of sleep each night. Each stage brings us into deeper sleep. On most nights, we go through these stages four or five times.

Teacher: Four stages of sleep. I wonder what they are.

> Most dreaming takes place during the fourth stage, which is called REM. REM sleep lasts from five to twenty minutes at a time. During REM sleep, the body is so limp that if anybody tried to wake you up, you would not be able to move for quite a few seconds.

Teacher: I wonder what REM means. They don't tell you here. The part about the body being limp is neat. Did that ever happen to you?

Student: I remember one time when I woke up from a really wild dream and couldn't move at all. I thought my dream was coming true.

Teacher: There's one paragraph left. Why don't you read it and stop to tell me what you're thinking after each sentence.

> People do not sleep "like a log." We move in our sleep as many as twenty to forty-five times every night. Much of this turning happens when our bodies are moving from one stage of sleep into the next. If we did not move at all during the time that we sleep, we could become quite sick.

From "Sleeping," in Book 2 of the *Challenger* Adult Reading Series, by Corea Murphy, New Readers Press, 1985, pp. 62–63.

Student: You said you don't move all night, but this says people move around a lot. It says we move 20 to 45 times a night. You could get tired from all that tossing and turning. Do you think you'd really get sick if you didn't move? I'd like to know more about that.

Teacher: Well done! Now you're really thinking while you read. When you do that, you'll understand better and remember much more.

Decoding

Instruction in phonics skills can occur during teachable moments. When an error pattern interferes with reading, a teacher introduces the student to the sound-symbol relationship.

The Moment

While reading to the teacher, a student couldn't decode two words that contained the digraph *ai*. This pattern of errors could indicate that the student did not know the sound for *ai*. The teacher decides to find out.

> Although I graduated from high school, I didn't think I could read well. So I was afraid to look for a job.
>
> I was afraid of the paper work that comes with some jobs. I worked as a waitress, but it's not good money.

From "Looking Ahead," by Bea Waltman, in *First Impressions,* New Readers Press, 1992. Reprinted by permission of the author.

Student: (Reading) "Although I grade . . . graduated from high school, I didn't think I could read well. So I was . . . angry? . . . to look for a job." No, that doesn't make sense. "So I was . . ."

Teacher: *Angry* is not a bad guess. The word is *afraid.*

Student: Oh. "So I was afraid to look for a job. I was . . . afraid of the paper work that comes with some jobs. I worked as a . . ."

Teacher: What parts of it can you sound out?

Student: It begins with /w/ . . . I'm still not sure.

Teacher: That's a good start. Let's learn about this vowel sound.

The Intervention

To help the student learn the long *a* sound for *ai*, the teacher lists a few simple words with the *ai* spelling for long *a*. Using the list, he guides the student in discovering the connection between the sound and the letters.

Teacher: These words have the same vowel sound as the first vowel in the word you're reading. Which ones can you read?

> rain
>
> paid
>
> brain
>
> paint

Student: "Rain, paid, br——"

Teacher: That's *brain.* And the last one?

Student: "Paint."

Teacher: Great! Now, what vowel letters do you see in these words?

Student: *A* and *i*. They all have *ai* together in the word.

Teacher: Good. Now let's read the first word in the list again.

Student: "Rain."

Teacher: Yes. What vowel sound do you hear in *rain?*

Student: /r/ . . . /ā/ . . . /n/. Sounds like a long *a*.

Teacher: Exactly. What vowel sound do you hear in the other words?

Student: "Paid, brain, paint. . . ." They all have the long *a* sound.

Teacher: And which letters are making the long *a* sound?

Student: *A* and *i* together?

Teacher: Exactly. When you see *ai* in a word, it's pronounced /ā/. Just like in the word *afraid* that you read before. Now, go back to where you left off. See if you can figure out the word now.

Student: "I worked as a wait . . . waitress, but it's not good money."

Teacher: Good job. Which of the *ai* words that we studied do you think would help you remember *ai* most easily? It can be a key word to help you remember how to read other *ai* words in the future.

Student: I think I'll remember *rain*. I'll write it in my notebook so I can study it at home.

NOTES ————————

I introduced ai to Bobbie. She chose rain as her key word. I added ai to the list of phonics elements to practice with her.

Blending

Blending involves identifying sounds within a word and bringing them together to read the word. When a student sounds out most parts of a word, but is still unable to read the whole word, the teacher shows him how to focus on the sequence of sounds within the word, by using a "backward buildup" strategy.

The Moment

During oral reading, the teacher notices that the student is having trouble combining the sounds to make a word. She decides to show him a strategy to help him blend. She writes out a couple of sentences for him to read.

> Sometimes children mistreat pets. They are not old enough to understand how much care an animal demands.

Student: "Sometimes children mis . . . mistake pets."

Teacher: Does that make sense to you?

Student: No, not really.

Teacher: Let's take a closer look at the word. What parts of it do you know? What are the sounds in the word?

Student: Well, the first part is *mis*. And there are two *t*'s. They would say /t/. And the *r* is /r/.

Teacher: Good. And how about the vowel sound?

Student: *Ea* would sound like /ē/ in *eat*.

Teacher: Great. You have all the sounds; now let's see if you can put them together. Reread the sentence and see what word with those sounds would make sense there.

Student: "Sometimes children mist . . . eat"? I'm drawing a blank.

The Intervention

The teacher shows the student a backward buildup approach. Using an index card, she covers the front part of the word. The student reads the part that is exposed. The teacher moves the index card forward one letter at a time. With each move, the student reads the uncovered part of the word.

Teacher: Let's try this. I'm going to cover the front part of the word. I want you to read the part that's showing. Maybe this will help you put it all together.

Student: That's "eat."

Teacher: OK. Good. (Uncovering *r*.) Now, what does it say?

Student: "R . . . reat"?

Teacher: Exactly right. (Uncovering *t*.) What does it say now?

Student: "T . . . reat. Treat."
Teacher: You bet. Can you read the whole word now?
Student: Oh, it says "mistreat."

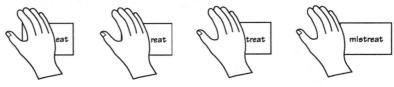

Teacher: Great. Now, try reading the sentence again.
Student: "Sometimes children mistreat pets."
Teacher: Can you think of an example of that?
Student: Maybe they forget to feed them.
Teacher: That's a good example. Let's continue reading.
Student: "They are not old enough to understand how much care an animal de . . . dem . . ." I'm not getting it.
Teacher: What sounds do you recognize in the word?
Student: The first part says /de/, I think. Then there's /m/ . . . "demonstrate"? No, I'm just guessing now.
Teacher: Let's try the same strategy as before. Cover up the first part of the word, and show only a vowel and the letters that come after it.
Student: It says, "and." I mean, "ands." I'll move the card again. Now it reads, "mands." Oh, it's "demands." I don't know why I couldn't see that the first time. I knew all the sounds but couldn't quite get it.

Teacher: And that's exactly when you can use this backward buildup. It helps you focus and bring the sounds together so you can read the word.

NOTES ————————————

Bob needed help blending. I
showed him how to do backward
buildup. It helped him.

CHAPTER 6 PATHWAYS TO WRITING

"Do you write?"

How you respond to that question has much to do with your perception of what writing is. Do you write novels or plays? Short stories or poems? Maybe not. How about letters, notes, memos, shopping lists, or personal checks? Unless we earn our living by writing, most of us barely notice the writing we do.

Unfortunately, many people have discomfort with, even a fear of, writing. They think that writing requires some kind of special knowledge possessed by only an elite few. One of the most important things we do as teachers is help change these attitudes.

What do we know about writing? People learn to write by writing. Adult learners need to write whenever there's an opportunity. The form and content of the writing should be governed by students' needs and wants. Avoiding writing only serves to mystify the process. If we write along with our students, we can experience writing together in a relaxing, personally gratifying way.

Writing reinforces reading, and should begin at the start of reading instruction. Reading occurs during writing. We read as we write, share, and comment on each other's writings. Reading and writing are two sides of the communication that goes on in written language.

Writing is also a way of recording; it is an external memory. Through writing we keep track of things and shape the past and future. Writing is private as well as public, mundane as well as creative.

This chapter contains suggestions for bringing writing into instruction by using writing as a personal tool, doing journal writing, freewriting, and directed writing, and sharing reading to learn effective writing.

Writing as a Personal Tool

First and foremost, writing is a personal tool for communication and survival. Proficient writers use writing for personal notes, business transactions, personal organization, and social communication. Since personal writing is for the student's own use, it can be a positive experience involving no editing or rewriting unless the student wishes. As they succeed in meeting their immediate needs, students become willing to explore other uses for writing.

Process:
> Begin with needs

> Expand to wants

> Broaden horizons

Begin with needs

Identify the adult learners' personal needs and desires for writing. Isolate the most immediate needs and work on those first.

> **Teacher:** What kinds of writing do you have to do in your lives?
>
> **Students:** Sign my name to get my child into school. Keep a medicine diary to give the doctor. Write checks to pay for household items.
>
> **Teacher:** OK. There is a lot of writing we can do to help with all those things. We can practice writing signatures until you write one you like. Bring in a notebook to start the medical diary. We can make a list of words you will need for it. I have some old checks we can use for check writing practice, too.

Expand to wants

Move on to the kinds of writing the learners want to do.

> **Teacher:** What would you like to write?
>
> **Students:** Birthday cards. Recipes. Bible verses. Letters.
>
> **Teacher:** Great. We can bring in cards and postcards. Let's write phrases together, and you can copy them. We can also address the envelopes.

Broaden horizons

As you share ways that writing can be used, students may become interested in keeping a date book, an address book, or making shopping lists. In class, students can do their own record keeping.

Journal Writing

Journal writing is a good way to get students into the flow of writing. Journal writing is done regularly, either daily or weekly. In journal writing, the writer is in charge and does not have to worry about what or how she writes. A journal is not the place to edit or correct writing. Journal writing can be done at home and in class. Students can use any notebook as a journal. You may need to reassure students that their journals are their own and will not be judged.

Types of Journals

A personal journal

The writer notes anything of interest. Some writers use journals as accounts of the day. Others use them to sort through difficult times in life, to deal with issues and changes. Journals serve as a safe outlet for thoughts and emotions. Many people separate their journals into two parts: a confidential part for their eyes only, and a public part that they share with others.

Before reading a student's personal journal, make sure you and the student are comfortable with your doing so. Reach an understanding about how to handle any sensitive topics in the journal.

A dialogue journal

This is a person-to-person conversation in writing. The writer gives the journal to the reader, who reads the entries and comments on them. The writer responds with new entries. Comments should relate to content, not evaluate or correct the writing. The teacher and student are "conversing" on equal ground as two correspondents. Sometimes, students and teachers exchange journals, each reading and responding to the other person's journal.

A directed journal

A journal entry can be directed at a particular issue or question. The writing can be reviewed by the teacher, shared with the class, or kept by the students. Many teachers use directed journals to begin or end a class. They pose a question for students to consider, or ask students to provide an assessment or make suggestions. Directed journals are valuable for concluding activities. Students can make notes of what they learned, tie what they have learned to their own lives, or try out new ideas or ways of writing.

Freewriting

Freewriting means putting pen to paper and writing continuously for several minutes. The emphasis is on the act of writing rather than on the content. The writing can wander anywhere, to any topic. A writer could begin writing about a newspaper article and end by repeating the words to a song. There is no censor in freewriting.

Freewriting is a way to brainstorm ideas in writing. It can be used to develop ideas before writing an essay or a poem, or before beginning to study a new topic. Freewriting is also an excellent way to help reluctant writers become comfortable with writing.

Process:
- Introduce freewriting
- Give a writing prompt if needed
- Let students write
- Call time
- Provide closure

Introduce freewriting

The point of freewriting is to experience the act of writing without censorship. The writing does not have to produce any usable content, and no one else needs to see what has been written. There are only two rules: (1) there is a set time limit for the activity (three to five minutes), and (2) the writing should be continuous.

Teacher: Write for the next five minutes. Keep on writing. Don't stop. Write about anything that comes to mind. Let your mind wander. Let the writing create surprises for you just as talking does.

Give a writing prompt if needed

Sometimes, adults do not respond well to freewriting because they don't see it as important or connected to anything. Providing a topic as an initial focus can help get students to start writing. Choose any topic that you think will easily generate writing.

Teacher: Look at this flower. Focus on it for a minute. Then, write whatever comes to mind. Don't worry about grammar or spelling. Just write.

Let students write

Encourage students to write for the allotted time without stopping. If they get stuck, they can recopy the line before, repeat a word over and over again, write song lyrics, or write about not having anything to write about. Eventually new ideas will come to them.

Call time

Stop the writing on time. If students know that there are boundaries to the exercise, they are likely to be willing to participate again.

Provide closure

Students can read over their freewriting to see if there are any phrases or ideas they want to keep or share with the group. You might ask if anyone would like to share something or if anyone raised any questions in their writing that they would like to bring to the group. Or you might just call time and move straight from the writing to the topic at hand.

Directed Writing

In directed writing, students are asked to respond to a writing prompt and write for 5–15 minutes about a particular topic or answer a specific question. Unlike freewriting, directed writing focuses on a specific topic and is usually tied to another part of a lesson. This activity provides a way for students to confer on paper with their teacher and other students. When students have finished writing, they can share their responses and write comments. If they are composing on computers, students can move to other students' computers, read what is on the screen, and type their comments. Two or three people can comment on each person's writing.

You and your students can create all kinds of writing prompts. Some types of prompts that are commonly used in instruction ask for a response to reading, summary and recall, analysis, evaluation, or hypothesizing.

Types of Prompts

Reading response

Prompts can ask for a personal response to reading. To welcome diverse views, these prompts are usually open-ended:

> What did you think about that short story?
>
> Who was your favorite character? What did you like about him/her?
>
> How would you relate this to your own life?
>
> How is your own experience similar to or different from this?
>
> If you could talk to the author, what would you say?

Summary and recall

To check for understanding, prompts can ask for summary and recall:

> What was the most important information?
>
> Retell this piece in your own words.
>
> Think of yourself as an expert on this subject. Tell us what we need to know.

Analysis

To examine information critically, prompts can ask for analysis:

> What do you think went wrong?
>
> Why do you think they behaved in this way?
>
> Why do you think the writer feels that way?
>
> In what ways do you agree or disagree? Why?
>
> What do the two have in common? How are they different?

Evaluation

To evaluate, prompts can ask for a judgment:

> Which character is the most admirable? Why?
>
> What did you learn about the subject from doing this assignment?
>
> What did you learn about how to read from doing this assignment?

Who would you recommend this book to? Why?

Which activities do you recommend we use again?

Hypothesizing

To hypothesize, prompts can ask supposition questions. To look at things in a different way, ask unusual association questions:

If you could change one thing, what would it be?

In the future, how might this change the way we live?

If you were Ann Landers, what advice would you give?

If the people you read about could be together in the same room, what conversation might they have?

What do you think might have happened if . . . ?

Reading for Writing

As students become more comfortable reading and writing, they are more likely to see reading as a resource for themselves as writers. Effective writing usually begins and ends well, has a purpose, is clearly written, and is memorable. These are qualities students can recognize, discuss, and strive for in their own writing.

On a regular basis, you and your students can spend a few minutes discussing good writing that you have come across in your reading. These discussions give students the opportunity to assess for themselves what makes writing effective. They also allow you to introduce terminology for thinking and talking about writing, and they strengthen the learners' views of themselves as readers who write and writers who read.

Process:
- Share the reading selection
- Be specific about what you liked
- Savor the flavor

Share the reading selection

Invite students to share interesting writing that they come across in their reading. It may be a sentence, paragraph, or very short selection that can be read aloud. If you are focusing on a particular type of text for reading or writing instruction, you may want to bring in examples of that type of writing. Ask students for their honest responses to the writing. Let them know that all opinions are welcome.

Be specific about what you liked

Point out particular qualities or wording that you like and try to express why you find them appealing.

As you and your students talk, introduce writing terms for the concepts:

Content: "The author had interesting things to say."

Development of ideas: "She gave examples so I got her point."

Style: "She wrote like she was talking to me. It was nice and plain."

Details: "She described the man so I knew what he looked like."

Freshness of language: "She made it fun to read."

Savor the flavor

Reread the selection or a few lines that you really enjoy. End the activity with the experience of the writing fresh in your minds.

CHAPTER 7 THE WRITING PROCESS

I sit at my table to write this introduction to the writing process. Around me are books and articles—I'm hoping for inspiration. I sit and think, staring out the window. I jot down some notes—reread my outline, and think about my experiences writing and teaching writing. I think of my students—past and present—how our work together will shape these pages. I do freewriting—spilling out stuff fast for five minutes—read it over—underline some surprises and ideas to pursue. I read some bits from the material around me—thinking: How do I write about the writing process in such a short space when others have taken whole books? I stare out the window again. This is so hard. I write some more—points from my reading I want to hit. I try several diagrams to illustrate the process—read what I've written—fix some spelling. I cross out a few phrases and substitute some words I like better. They fit. I remember who I'm writing for—wondering if this will make sense. OK. I've planned enough—now I'm ready for my first draft.

Writing is a process: Thinking, collecting ideas, drafting, reading, collecting more ideas, thinking more, rewriting, sharing, and editing. Its stages intertwine. We move among them when we write. These are not separate steps that lead directly to the next. Rather, during each stage, one kind of event is primary, while others play a smaller role. As we develop a piece of writing we do the following:

Plan: Think about what to write and who the writing is for. Collect ideas. Organize information.

Draft: Write thoughts down. Concern is for content not conventions.

Share: Give the writing to someone else to read, or read it to an audience. Read it aloud. Hear how it sounds. Ask for specific feedback.

Revise: Make changes to clarify and focus the piece.

Edit: Make the writing readable for others. Take conventions into consideration.

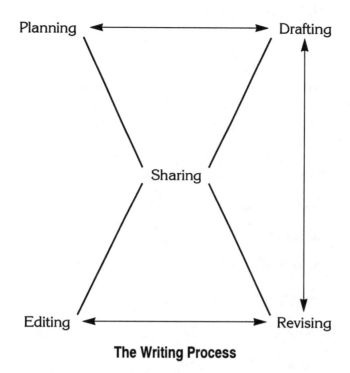

The Writing Process

To help adult learners become independent writers, we teach the behaviors and practices that experienced writers use. As students become aware of the process they use when writing, and develop strategies to help them during each stage, they begin to think of themselves as writers. They choose their own topics and write for real purposes. They write whole pieces just as experienced writers do, and schedule time to write regularly. As teachers, we provide an environment in which we are fellow writers. We act as a supportive audience. We respect students' language and don't impose our own. And we provide opportunities for students to publish their writing so they can see it in print.

The writing process is fundamental to all kinds of writing intended for communication. Students can learn to engage in the writing process whenever they write on a topic that they have a commitment to. It is essential that students write on subjects that are important to them. Writing skills are best learned when students are engaged in the writing, when they have a strong purpose and need for learning the skills.

This chapter is about implementing the writing process. A section on implementation is followed by a general activity for introducing the writing process and a sample activity showing a student engaging in the writing process. Next are general activities for using it in letter writing and in writing an autobiography.

Implementing the Writing Process

By engaging in the writing process, students gain the flexibility and control over writing that is the hallmark of experienced writers. They gain the ability to develop a piece of writing to the level they desire for a given task. This section describes the stages of the writing process and suggests ways to organize the writing environment.

Key Events:

Plan

Draft

Conference

Share

Revise

Edit

Publish

Plan

During the planning stage, writers keep in mind that they can still change everything they write. They are more concerned with generating ideas and looking at how the ideas might fit together than writing complete sentences or doing a lot of writing.

First, writers choose a topic. Students should choose a topic of genuine interest so they can maintain their interest even when the writing gets difficult. Students will take greater risks with language, write more, and find it easier to learn new skills if they are interested in what they are writing. Students can brainstorm ideas and keep an ongoing list of writing ideas. When looking for a topic, they can refer to their list of ideas for writing. (See the Ideas for Writing handout on page 100.)

There are several planning techniques that help writers collect and organize ideas in ways that will help them write the first draft. Planning strategies include: talking, brainstorming, doing a mind map, making a timeline, and freewriting. Writers use some or all of these techniques whenever they are planning to write.

Talking. By talking with others, writers can explore and develop their ideas. Through conversation they clarify what they are thinking about and what they know and don't know. They can put ideas into words that they might want to use when they write. Some writers always keep paper and pen at hand. They write down any ideas they like that come out of the conversation.

Brainstorming. This is a good technique to use whenever writers need to free themselves up to think of ideas. In brainstorming, many ideas flow quickly and in no particular order. Ideas are not evaluated or censored. All the ideas are listed. Afterward, the writer looks at the list and considers which ideas fit together and which ones to use.

Doing a mind map. Writers use mind maps to chunk ideas together and explore how ideas relate to each other. Mind mapping is a good activity to follow brainstorming. The writer decides which ideas belong together and how they fit with other ideas.

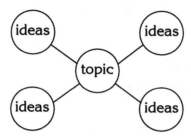

Making a timeline. Like a mind map, a timeline is also an organizer. It can help the writer plan a logical order in which one event follows another. Timelines are useful for planning stories, histories, or biographies. Students can fill in a timeline to show the order in which things happened or the steps of the process.

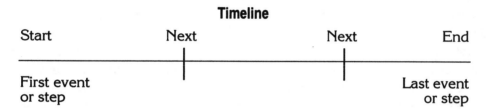

Freewriting. Freewriting can be a warm-up for a first draft. Writers let their thoughts flow freely while they write. They just start writing and keep writing for a few minutes. Then they read what they've written to see which ideas or words might be worth using in their writing.

Draft

During the drafting stage writers need blocks of uninterrupted writing time. Your role is that of observer and facilitator. You can watch while your students write and be ready to confer if someone needs help. This is also a time for you to write, since this provides a model for students and lets them see you as a writer going through the same struggles and stages they are going through.

When students are new to the writing process, it helps to have them look at some first drafts that others have produced. You can share a draft of your own, or invite outside writers to visit and bring some of their first drafts. Point out how messy and incomplete a first draft looks. Some words are crossed out and others written over the top. Remind students not to worry about spelling or punctuation during the drafting stage.

During the drafting stage, students may need help to keep going. Reading over what they have written so far is one good strategy you can suggest. Another is talking. Conferring briefly with students and helping them talk about their subject can help get their ideas flowing again.

Drafting Stage Reminders

- Double-space your drafts so you have room to make changes later.
- If you get stuck while writing the draft, read it over, or talk to someone about your topic.
- If you have trouble with spelling:
  Use invented spelling.
  Use dashes to indicate words or parts of words.
  Ask for help (but not too often or you might get sidetracked).
- You can correct spelling and punctuation during the editing stage. Don't be concerned with them now.

Conference

Be available for brief conferences with students as they work. During all stages of the writing process, your students might need help. They might be searching unsuccessfully for a particular word or phrase, or feeling that they are stuck and can't move their writing forward. Sometimes they might need to get up and walk around. When students confer with you, try to keep the conferences brief. Find out what the issue is and suggest a strategy to deal with that issue. Documenting the questions students raise and the problems they encounter, as well as your responses to them, provides you with a record of your instructional interventions. The list of items may suggest topics for future mini-lessons. (See the Writing Conference Record on page 101.)

Share

Sharing is a vital part of the writing process. Sharing helps students learn to think about their writing critically, as a piece of work in progress that they own and can develop. During sharing, the writer reads his writing aloud to another student who is the audience. Sharing can take place at many points during the writing process. Brief sharing is done informally during writing and in writing conferences. Planned sharing can be done after drafting, revising, and with the final product. Writers want to learn from the audience. They want to know if their point is getting across, if anything is confusing, and why the audience likes or doesn't like it. As the audience, students learn how to give helpful feedback.

Learning how to give and respond to constructive criticism is important for new writers. Typically, new writers are afraid of being criticized, and the audience fears being either too critical or not critical enough. Productive sharing takes practice. A good way for students to learn how to share effectively is to observe a writer sharing work with an audience. Students can observe an actual sharing session or a role play. A feedback guide used during sharing sessions can serve as a helpful reminder for both the writer and the listener. (See the Writer's Feedback Guide on page 102.)

Elements for Helpful Sharing

The author shares the writing.

The author asks for specific feedback.

The audience answers the author's questions.

The audience retells the piece, so the author knows what was heard.

The audience points out what worked and what was unclear.

The audience tells what, if anything, it wants to hear more of.

The author asks the audience any further questions and the audience answers.

Revise

Revise means "seeing again." Not every piece of writing needs revision, but most writers want to revise writing that others will see. Revising involves carefully reading, changing, and rereading a draft to organize and clarify the writing. It does not involve correcting grammar and punctuation. Students should understand the difference between revising and editing.

After sharing or reading over a draft, writers make changes based on the feedback they get from others as well as on what they hear internally as they read their own writing. They work to make the meaning clear. They look at the piece as a whole and also at individual wording for improvements in content, organization, or wording. Students can share their revised drafts.

To demonstrate revising, you can show students how you revise your own draft. Put your draft on the board or a flip chart. Think aloud, making comments to yourself, as you revise what you have written. Show students how to cross out words and draw arrows to indicate inserted text. Ask them to name the strategies that you used and to recall the questions you asked yourself. Discuss the effects the revisions have on the piece. Record what students say. Have students try out the same strategies and discuss what they did.

Revising Strategies

- Look at the piece as a whole as well as at where each part fits. Move parts to a new place to create an effect, or to make a piece clearer or more logical. Ask these questions:
    Am I making the points I want the reader to get?
    Do the ideas follow each other?
    If I were to move this here, what would happen?

- Add words and sentences to make the writing clearer or to expand it. Ask yourself:
    Is there enough here to make my point?
    What do I need to add to explain what I mean?
    What examples will show what I mean?
    If I add this, what happens?

- Take out words and sentences if they are confusing or inaccurate. Ask yourself:
    - Does this make sense to me?
    - Does this really say what I want it to say?
    - If I take this out, what happens?
- Replace specific words and phrases to make the writing clearer. Ask yourself:
    - What effect does this wording have?
    - Have I used the best words?
    - What words would be more interesting or more exact?

Edit

Writers edit to make their meaning clear to the reader by using the conventions of written English. The writer decides the extent to which a piece of writing is edited. The amount of editing usually depends on the purpose of the writing. Lists, notes, or a journal or diary are usually not edited. A letter to a friend or family member may need basic editing—commas and periods to indicate pauses, and spelling that is close to the sound of the word. A business letter should have all the standard mechanics in place.

Editing is also a chance to clarify relationships between ideas by adding transition and signal words. Students can share their edited versions.

Introducing editing skills as they are needed for a piece of writing helps students see that these skills are useful for clarifying meaning. Skills can be introduced during a teachable moment in a writing conference and then be taught more formally in a mini-lesson. Focusing on one or two editing skills at a time makes learning the skills more manageable.

Editing Checklist

Carefully read what you've written. Check that you have:

- Capital letters to start each sentence
- Period or question mark at the end of each sentence
- Correct spelling
- Formal grammar usage:
    - Correct verb tense
    - Agreement between subject and verb (both plural or singular)
- Guide words to help the reader:
    - Words to provide transition (first, next, finally)
    - Words to signal information (for example, one reason is . . .)

Publish

Publishing brings completeness to the writing process. One of the purposes of writing is to be read, but the reason to publish is best said by adult learners themselves: "This book means that I have value, that what I have to say is important."

"I've always wanted to write my own piece, and here it is."

"When I publish my work, I'm educating people, telling them what my experience is like."

Students can publish in various ways. Sending a letter to a friend, a potential employer, or a local newspaper, or submitting pieces to the school newsletter are all forms of publishing. Your class can also publish books written by students. A book can contain selections on different topics, selections on the same topic, or a collection of writings by one student.

Introduce adult learners to possibilities for publishing and ask what they would like to do. If you have access to the necessary computer equipment, desktop publishing is an excellent activity. It provides opportunities to learn about using computers, doing page and book layouts, cover design, and creating captions and titles. Publishing is also an incentive for writing and for setting and meeting deadlines. If you do not have word-processing equipment, the writing can be typed or copied carefully by hand and bound or displayed in various ways.

Guidelines for Implementing the Writing Process

Use the writing process in the context of meaningful writing.

Let students write often in blocks of uninterrupted writing time.

Allow more time for actual writing than for skill practice.

Provide opportunities to publish students' writings.

Model what you do by writing and sharing your work.

Allow students to select topics that will sustain their interest.

Encourage students' voices to come through in their writing.

Talk about the process, about what students are doing as they write.

Let students decide when a piece is finished or when to stop.

Ideas for Writing

Name _____   Date started _____

Directions: Write down things that you think might be interesting to write about.

Interesting people	Interesting places
Images: Things I've seen	**Words: Things I've heard or read**
Events: Things that have happened	**Ideas: Things I've thought about**
Questions: Things I want to know	**Problems: Things I want to change**

Writing Conference Record

Student Name _____

Date	Piece of Writing	Points Discussed	Notes for Further Discussion

Writer's Feedback Guide

Directions: Read this list before sharing. Then, check (✓) the things you did while sharing your writing. Remember: You don't have to do each item. Do only what you need for helpful sharing.

For the Author:

_____ Tell the audience what you want them to listen for.

_____ Ask questions: Does this sound better than this?

_____ Ask what else the audience wants to know.

_____ Take notes on what the audience says.

_____ Take notes on what you wanted to fix as you read to the audience.

For the Audience:

_____ Retell the piece in your own words.

_____ Respond to what the author asked you to listen for.

_____ Is everything clear? If not, say what isn't.

_____ Tell what parts you liked best and why.

_____ Tell what you'd like to hear more about.

Introducing the Writing Process

This is an activity to introduce students to the writing process before they begin their first piece of sustained writing. Developing a piece of writing can extend for several sessions. Having a complete picture of the writing process serves as a guide along the way.

Purpose: To provide students with an overview of the writing process.

Materials: A variety of paper (lined and unlined), pens, pencils, markers, dictionaries appropriate to the students' levels, a thesaurus, and a computer with word-processing software and storage (optional).

Process:

> Talk about writing

> Identify stages of the writing process

> Provide a guide to the writing process

Try to give students plenty of physical space where they will be writing. When space is limited, it is helpful if you develop ground rules about talking, humming, or walking around, so people can move around and get comfortable without disturbing others.

Students should have their own place to store their papers, such as a manila folder, a box, or a binder. Encourage students to keep all their notes, drafts, revisions, conference records, and checklists for each project. This can help students notice the improvement they make over time and provide bases for building portfolios.

Computers are valuable for both composing and publishing. Drafting, revising, and editing are much more fluid when using a computer than when writing by hand or typing.

Talk about writing

To help students think of themselves as writers and feel comfortable about writing, discuss what they think writing is, what they do when they write, and what they would like to do. Set some writing goals. As the students learn more about writing, provide opportunities for students to add other writing goals. You will notice that students' thoughts and feelings about writing often do change as they become more experienced.

At an initial meeting, present the class with a set of questions on a flip chart or chalkboard or as a handout.

> What is writing?
> How do you feel about writing?
> Why do people write?
> Why do you write?
> What do you write now?
> What do you want to be able to do with writing?

Teacher: We want to think about and share what we know about writing. It will help us understand what we mean when we say "writing" and allow us to look at what we do when we write. Here are some questions to help. Let's discuss each question, and I'll record what you say on the board.

Students may suggest items such as these:

> **What is writing?**
>
> spelling   make it make sense
> punctuation   feelings
> you get an idea   clarity
> concentration   a joy when you do it right
> beginning, middle, end

Teacher: Yes. All these things are parts of writing. It's a complex process. Write down what you say now about writing, and put it in your working folder. Keep it as a record to see if your ideas change over time and if you are meeting your goals.

Identify stages of the writing process

Ask students to talk about what they do when they write. As they describe the process they use, introduce the names of the stages. Help students describe planning, drafting, sharing, revising, and editing. Tell students what writing is like for you and what you do when you write. From the information discussed, make a list of items for each stage of the process.

Teacher: What do you do when you write? What happens first?

Student: When I have to write a letter to my kid's school, I sit down and chew my pen, then I write down what I want to say. I read it over. I give it to my friend to look over. If she says it's OK, I send it. If she sees something not right, I do it over again.

Teacher: Each of the things that you did are what we all do when we write. All the different stages are called the writing process. The first thing you did was think about what you wanted to say. That's called planning. Then you sat down and wrote the whole thing all the way through. That's called writing a draft. You gave your draft to your friend to read and give you feedback. That's called sharing. Did you ask her to read it aloud so you could hear it? When your friend said there were things you needed to change to make it easier to follow, you changed it. That's called revising. You probably also checked for spelling and periods, right? That's called editing.

Sometimes, we do all these stages in our heads really fast. We often don't even know we're doing them. It depends on what we are writing. When I have to prepare a paper with a lot of information in it, I spend a lot of time planning, reading articles, and talking to experts. Then I figure out how to organize my paper, what ideas I want to use, and where I want to put them. That's all before I write a draft. But when I write a fictional story, I might start by just freewriting to see where my mind takes me. So it depends.

Provide a guide to the writing process

Many ideas can result from talking about the writing process. You can use the list of ideas to make a poster outlining the writing process. Referring to the poster at the start of each writing activity reminds students where they are and what they might expect to be happening. Students may also want to use a process guide for reference. (See the Writing Process Guide on page 106.)

Writing Process Guide

Directions: You can refer to this when you write.

Plan

Think about what you want to write.

How?   Choose a topic: Make a topic list.

Collect your ideas: Read. Talk to others. Brainstorm. Freewrite.

Organize your information: Which ideas go together? What is the general order? Make a mind map. Make a timeline. Outline.

Draft

Write your thoughts down. Don't worry about spelling or punctuation.

How?   Give yourself plenty of writing time.

Read over what you've written to help you write more.

Use invented spelling or draw lines in place of words.

Talk to someone if you get stuck.

Share

Read your writing to an audience to hear how it sounds aloud.

How?   Ask for specific feedback. Ask: "How does this part sound? Which sounds better, this or this?"

Take notes on feedback you get.

Revise

Read your writing. Look at it as a reader not as the writer.

How?   Think about the whole and the parts. Does everything fit together?

Ask yourself: Does it make sense? Is it clear? Do ideas logically follow each other? Are transitions clear?

Move parts of the text around. Add words or sentences. Delete words or sentences.

Try different words.

Edit

Read your writing to make sure it is readable by others.

How?   Check the spelling, punctuation, grammar, and usage.

Use the skills you know.

Check the wording for transition and signal words.

Share with another writer and check each other's writing.

Prepare a clean final copy.

Sample: Introducing the Writing Process

Engaging in the Writing Process

As part of writing instruction in a workplace literacy class, a student chose to write a personal narrative. In doing so, she learned about the stages of the writing process, increased her writing skills, broadened her understanding of writing, and gained confidence in herself as a writer.

Process:
- Talk about writing
- Plan
- Draft
- Share
- Revise
- Edit
- Publish

Talk about writing

As he had with other students in the class, the teacher briefly spoke with this student about her writing goals and the kinds of writing she did.

Teacher: Lynn, what are your goals for writing?
Student: I want to improve my penmanship, spelling, and vocabulary.
Teacher: What kinds of writing do you do?
Student: I just write messages; and now I started a journal for class.

Plan

The teacher helped the student find a general topic and suggested ways to explore ideas she could write about.

Teacher: The first thing to do is find a subject.
Student: I want to work on a book about myself. But it's too much.
Teacher: Well, you've got your subject. To collect ideas, you can brainstorm and make a mind map. Or you could freewrite.
Student: I'll freewrite.

The student wrote the following:

> I want to write a book about my life and my family and when I was a little and and how I am today so I think I will write when I was about one or two years old I remember my mother had a fight with her boyfriend and he was outside and try to get in are house my mother warrant him not to get in and she was no play, with him at all and he try to get in and my mother got her gun and shot him with it. She called the polices and they did not take my mother to jail her boyfriend was not death and he never try to beat my mother no more or fight with my mother anye more.

Draft

The student found that the freewriting had helped her connect quickly with her memories, but she didn't want to develop this story for other people to read. So she decided to continue writing until she got some more ideas. The teacher soon noticed that she had stopped writing. He helped the student talk about her subject and write down what she had said. This enabled the student to proceed and complete the draft.

Teacher: How do you want to use your freewriting to write the first draft?
Student: I don't know. I'll just keep writing, I guess.
Teacher: OK. We have 40 minutes to write the first draft. Get comfortable and begin when you're ready.

After a while, the teacher checked on the student to see how she was doing.

Teacher: How's it going?
Student: I'm stuck.
Teacher: What are you stuck on?
Student: I don't know what else to say.
Teacher: Well, what else do you remember about your childhood?
Student: Well, my brother Dennis always was mean.
Teacher: "My brother Dennis always was mean." Write that down. I'll repeat it for you.
Student: Oh. Yeah. I got it now. I'll write about my brother.

Draft 1 Student Writing:

> my brother was Dennis was mean to use. he use to make us sit on the floor to watch tv and he got to watch the TV in the Big Chair. What are mother was gone one time, he told my sister you sit on the floor to my sister chritine and she had to watch TV on the floor. but that day my brother sit in the chair bragin to use he was the king. and the wall in are stiling came down on top of his head. He look like he was white we all laugh so hard we coudnt breath my brother stoped siting over in the king chaired

Teacher: OK. Read it over to yourself and make any changes you want. Then we'll take a break and share our drafts.

Share

Because the class was new, the teacher helped the class learn how to share their writing. He and a volunteer student modeled a "bad" sharing and a "good" sharing.

Teacher: We're going to show you two examples of sharing. You decide which one is more helpful and why.

Role play 1

The author reads the piece.

Listener: That was good, I liked it.
Author: Thanks.

Role play 2

The author reads the piece.

Author: Could you tell what the problem was?
Listener: Yes. You said it and showed it. I didn't get the ending, though. You just stopped.

Then the class discussed the attributes of successful sharing.

Teacher: What was the difference between the first sharing and the second? Which one helped the author?

Students: The first one was bad, but the second one was helpful. In the first one, the author just read. But in the second, the author asked for specific feedback. It was more helpful when the listener answered the author's question. In the first role play, the listener just said he liked it. He didn't say why and the author didn't ask. It was better when the listener said why he liked it and what was confusing.

Then the class formed pairs and shared their writing.

Author: This is a story about my brother. (Reads story.) What do you think of him?

Listener: He sounds like he pushes everybody around. You did a good job telling the story. It was funny. But I didn't get some of the ways you used the words.

Revise

In a writing conference, the student and teacher discussed revising. Not all writing needs extensive revision. In short personal narratives, the writing is often organized in a straightforward way, so revisions tend to be at the word and sentence level. Here, the teacher helped the student revise by reading sentences to her and asking her if she was satisfied with them.

Teacher: Lynn, do you want to revise the story about your brother?

Student: Yes.

Teacher: I'll read and you listen for any problems. "My brother was Dennis was mean to us."

Student: That doesn't make sense. I say *was* too much.

Teacher: What would make sense?

Student: If I said it once. "My brother Dennis was mean to us."

Teacher: "He used to make us sit on the wood floor and he got to watch TV in the big chair."

Student: He hit us, too.

Teacher: Do you want to add that?

During the next writing activity, the student again examined her writing for possible revisions.

Teacher: Read your draft through one more time and underline any parts you aren't sure of or might want to change.

Student: "He told my sister you sit on the floor to my sister." That doesn't sound right.

Teacher: What would make that better?

Student: "He told my sister, you sit on the floor."

Teacher: Yes, that sounds better. Can you say why?

Student: I'm not sure.

Teacher: You had said the same thing twice. "He told my sister" and "to my sister" mean the same thing. You only needed it once.

Student: What about this? "But that day my brother sat in the chair braggin to us he was the king. The ceiling came down on top of his head."

Teacher: You have him bragging as usual and then something different happens. It's kind of suspenseful.

Student: Yeah, it was so sudden.

Teacher: Do you want to use that? *Sudden* is a good word. You can also say *suddenly* or *all of a sudden*.

Student: I like that, *all of a sudden*. Where would I put that?

Teacher: Use it like the word *but*. Put it between the things you are comparing, where you are showing the difference between what was happening before and what's happening now.

Draft 2 Student Writing:

My brother Dennis was mean to us. He use to make us sit on the wood floor to watch TV or he would hit us. He got to watch TV in the big chair. When our mother was gone one time, he told my sister, you sit on the floor. She had to watch TV on the floor. That day my brother sat in the chair braggin to us he was the king. But then, all of a sudden, The ceiling came down on top of his head. He look like he was white. We all laugh so hard we couldn't breath. My brother stoped siting over in the king chair.

Edit

The editing phase provides the context for teaching spelling, punctuation, grammatical usage, and other skills associated with formal written English.

The teacher had noticed that many students in the class did not consistently use -ed to mark past tense in verbs. He was planning a class mini-lesson on past tense. Here, he introduced the topic to this student.

Teacher: Lynn, now that you have revised your piece, we're ready to work on editing. What skills do you feel you need to work on?

Student: I don't know. What do you see?

Teacher: Well, let's talk a little about past tense. In writing, the verbs show the action. So you change the verbs to show when the action happens. With some verbs, the past tense changes how the word looks, like when you change *tell* to *told*. With other verbs, you make past tense by adding -ed to the end of the word. *Look* changes to *looked*. It's hard to hear the -ed when we talk, but it's easy to see the -ed in writing. In your piece, you sometimes show the past tense in the verbs and sometimes you don't. Let's go over the verbs together to see if you are making them past tense when you want them to be.

To prepare the work for publishing, the teacher completed the editing process for the student. Then the student made a final copy. The teacher kept track of the corrections he had made and briefly reviewed them with the student. Corrected drafts are helpful in teaching skills, since the student can easily notice the new additions to her text.

Draft 3 Student Writing:

> My brother's name is Dennis. He was mean to us. He used to make us sit on the wood floor to watch TV or he would hit us. He got to watch TV in the big chair. When our mother was gone one time, he told my sister Christine to sit on the floor. She had to watch TV on the floor. That day my brother sat in the chair bragging to us he was the King. But then, all of a sudden, the ceiling came down on top of his head. He looked like he was white. We all laughed so hard we couldn't breathe. My brother stopped sitting over in the king chair.

Publish

The teacher and student talked about opportunities for publishing.

Teacher: This is a nice piece. Later in the year the class could publish a book of writings, and if you want, you could submit this piece. There are also a few publishers who publish student writing. We could send them this piece if you'd like.

Student: That sounds good.

Teacher: OK. You'll need to write a cover letter to send with it. That could be the next writing you do.

Writing Letters

Letter writing is a practical activity and perhaps the most common form of writing to others that most adults do. Often, there is a tangible result, maybe a reply or a free product. Students can write personal letters and business letters in class.

Process:
> Give an overview
>
> Explain the parts of a letter
>
> Draft, revise, edit
>
> Prepare the envelope

Give an overview

Bring in a variety of letters to use as models for the kinds of letters that students want to write. Include letters that you've received or have written. Explain that when writing a letter, it's important to keep purpose and audience in mind. Introduce both personal letter writing and business letter writing.

Personal letter writing. People write personal letters to family and friends for everyday correspondence and to send messages on special occasions. Students can begin letter writing by writing to each other. Students can also exchange letters with students in other classes and programs.

Business letter writing. People write business letters to make requests, suggestions, and complaints. Government agencies and businesses are used to receiving letters of complaint or approval, and requests for information. Government policy can be affected by the kinds of letters politicians receive. Public opinion can be affected by letters to the editor. Students can write business letters as a class or for individual purposes.

Explain the parts of a letter

Explain that letters have a conventional form. Write out the basic form of letters and explain each part. Help students formulate their purpose in writing and the main message they want to communicate. Students may decide to write a personal letter or a business letter. Explain how to write each part of the letter.

Form of a personal letter	Form of a business letter
Your address and the date	Your address and the date
Greeting	Their address
Body	Greeting
Closing and signature	Introduction
	Body
	Conclusion
	Closing and signature

1. Identify the purpose and audience.

> **Teacher:** Why do you want to write this letter? Who are you going to send the letter to? How well do you know that person? Is this a letter to a friend or a business letter? In general, what do you want to say?

2. Explain how to write the date, addresses, and greeting.

> **Teacher:** In a personal letter, write your address and the date at the top of the page. You can write the name of the month or just use numbers. In a business letter, write the address of the person you are writing to also.
>
> If you are on a first-name basis with the person, write Dear (first name). Otherwise write Mr., Ms., Miss, or Mrs. You can also write a general greeting if you don't have the name of a specific person.

3. In a business letter, write an introduction.

> **Teacher:** Introduce yourself. Say why you are writing this letter. Say what you want the recipient to do or know. You might start with, "I am writing this letter because . . ."

4. Write the body of the letter. This is often a series of events telling the story behind the reason for writing or an argument giving your ideas and information to support them.

> **Teacher:** Give your message. Give details, explanations, and reasons.

5. In a business letter, write a conclusion.

> **Teacher:** In a business letter, you may want to thank the reader for the time and effort of acting on your request, and ask for a reply.

6. Close and sign the letter.

> **Teacher:** A common closing for a business letter is "Sincerely." Sign your whole name to a business letter. You may also want to give your phone number.

Draft, revise, edit

Students can now draft their letters. Then they should reread and revise as needed so that their message will be clear to the reader. Finally, students can edit for punctuation, spelling, and other surface features.

Prepare the envelope

Students who have not written many letters may need assistance with the layout of the envelope, the return address, and the number of stamps to use.

Writing an Autobiography

Even students who don't like most reading and writing activities are usually interested in writing an autobiography. It is an excellent way for students to produce a complete book, organized by chapters. People can get to know themselves and each other by writing and sharing stories about their lives.

Process:

> Introduce autobiography
>
> Plan, draft, and share
>
> Organize by chapters
>
> Revise and edit
>
> Publish and celebrate

Introduce autobiography

We all use stories to tell about our lives. You and your students can enjoy reading about other peoples' lives. Bring in biographies and autobiographies of famous people. Read the chapter headings. Look at the photographs. Note how the stories about people's lives often go in a timeline from birth to childhood to adulthood. Ask the students if they would like to write their autobiographies, perhaps with a view toward sharing and publishing them.

Plan, draft, and share

Ask students to talk about aspects of their lives that are interesting or important to them. As students talk about their own lives, some of the memories may be painful. If so, the group will need to be supportive. Ask students to name topics that were raised. Write each topic on the board.

Teacher: What kinds of things do we want to know about people and their lives?

Students: Marriage, birth, children, jobs, childhood, school days, summers, family, friends, first date, first love, sports, hobbies, church, hopes.

Ask students to write while their ideas are fresh in their minds. Form small groups or pairs to share drafts. Students read their drafts aloud. The writing partners ask questions or make comments to suggest areas they want to know more about. These questions help the writer expand and shape the writing. Students might also bring in pictures or mementos to stimulate ideas for writing.

Questions such as these help students develop their writing:

Can you tell me more about that person?

What did you think when that happened?

What did that mean to you?

What a great story. Were you surprised when that happened?

What was it like living there?

What do you want to do when your children are older?

Organize by chapters

As students write and talk over the course of several sessions, the writing may take a natural shape with each major event or aspect of life becoming a separate chapter. Some students may want to plan out their chapters first and then write using chapter headings as topics for writing.

Most students will organize their book chronologically, using a timeline to mark off major events. But students can also organize their book thematically:

> All the Best (My Best Job, My Best Friend, My Best Time, My Best Plan)
>
> Things I Know (The Hardest Lesson I Ever Learned, My Lessons in Love)

Whatever organization students choose at the beginning can be tentative and open to change until all the writing is done, since each new installment can provide an unexpected direction.

Revise and edit

As they go along, students will probably want to add or clarify points in response to questions and comments. When they are comfortable with what they have written and feel that they have done justice to their stories, they can begin editing. Students can read each other's manuscripts and indicate where they are having difficulty understanding the text. Problems may stem from spelling, or lack of punctuation or paragraphs.

After students have edited one another's writing, they will probably want you to check it. Many teachers correct spelling and punctuation before it is seen by an outside audience but leave usage and idiom in the student's voice. Be sensitive to students' wishes when you deal with editing, since this is their book.

Publish and celebrate

As much as possible, students should organize and produce the book. They can organize the chapters, write the headings and captions, make illustrations, and design the covers. Print copies for the student, teacher, and program. Finally, a celebration is in order. Students have written the stories of their lives. The accomplishment is something to celebrate.

CHAPTER 8 TEACHABLE MOMENTS IN WRITING

Teachable moments in writing are unplanned points during a writing activity when a missing piece of the puzzle surfaces as an opportunity for teaching. To make use of a teachable moment, we need to be alert to the learners' needs. We need to be flexible and ready to seize the opportunity.

Teaching something new about writing while the student is engaged in the writing process helps move the student forward. Taking advantage of teachable moments makes it clear to the learners that they are at the center of the learning process. An immediate response encourages students to continue to ask questions or make comments, which in turn enhances learning.

Teachable moments can occur during any stage of writing. They often happen during a writing conference, when a teacher consults with a student one-to-one. But sometimes, teachable moments arise during a group discussion, and those opportunities should be seized as well.

Teachable moments differ from mini-lessons in that they are unplanned. Needs that surface during teachable moments can become topics for formal instruction in mini-lessons.

There are three kinds of interventions you can do in a teachable moment:

1. Point out a strategy or skill the student is using by giving it a name, making it explicit. This helps the student gain control over the skill or strategy, so she can use it again when she needs it.

2. Focus on something the student is struggling with. Help her over the hump so she can continue her writing.

3. Introduce a new skill or strategy that the student needs in order to expand or enhance her writing.

This chapter has examples of teachable moments that can occur as students move through the stages of the writing process.

Finding a Starting Point

In the planning stage, a teacher helps a student find a topic to write about.

The Moment

A student who is struggling to find something to write about calls the teacher over for help. The teacher lets him know that he is free to write about whatever interests him. Since the student has some titles in mind, the teacher helps him find a topic by discussing his ideas for titles.

Student: I still don't know what to write about.
Teacher: I thought you were going to write about your neighborhood.
Student: I was, but I don't like that topic.
Teacher: What were some other ideas you had?
Student: I don't know. All I can think of are some titles.

The Intervention

Teacher: Titles? That might be a good way for you to find a subject. Go ahead and write down the titles you thought of. Then we'll look at them and see what happens. I'll check back with you in 10 minutes to see how it's going.

The teacher returns in 10 minutes as promised.

Student: OK—here's the list.

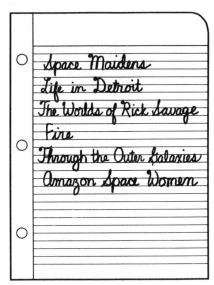

Teacher: Harry, this is great. What a list! So, who's this guy Rick Savage? I love the name.
Student: He's a science fiction guy, a space pirate.
Teacher: Why don't you write about him?
Student: You mean I can?
Teacher: Yes. This seems to be something you connect with, and that's what makes a subject good. Go for it. And keep this list of titles in your folder. If you get stuck again, go back to it. Listing possible titles seems to be a good way for you to find your topic.

Doing a Mind Map

In the planning stage, a student uses a mind map to begin exploring ideas.

The Moment

A student who knows the topic he wants to write about has made several attempts to start his draft. He needs a way to produce ideas for his topic. The teacher shows the student how to make a mind map to develop his ideas.

Student: I want to write on homelessness, but I don't know where to start.

The Intervention

Teacher: You chose a pretty big topic. Try to narrow it down. Let's make a mind map of all the things you are thinking about homelessness. Write the word *Homelessness* in the middle of the paper and circle it. That's your topic. When you think of homelessness, what comes to mind?

Student: Families.

Teacher: OK. What else?

Student: Shelters, begging.

Teacher: Now, put those words on the paper and show how they are connected to your topic. (Student writes.) Now, break down each part further. What comes to mind when you think of shelters?

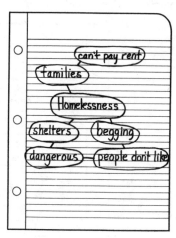

Teacher: What ideas do you get from this map?

Student: Well, people don't like homeless people. They don't like all that begging. But there's a lot of families that are homeless . . . OK. I can start.

Teacher: Good. Now, once you start writing, keep going. But if you get lost, you can look back at your map to use what's there or add more things.

Organizing with the W's

In the planning stage, a student uses a newspaper story as a model for writing.

The Moment

When a student asks for help with writing a report on a meeting she attended, the teacher helps her by using the organization of a news story as a model.

Student: I've got these notes on the city council meeting. But I'm not sure how to put them together.

Teacher: Well, let's see. You've got facts about what happened and then you give your opinion, too. What is your purpose for writing? Is it to give your opinion, or to report on the meeting, or both?

Student: I want to write an article like the newspapers. How do the newspaper writers do it?

The Intervention

Teacher: Let's take a look. Here's my newspaper. Find an article you think is similar to yours, and let's see if we can figure it out.

Student: Here's one reporting on a budget meeting.

Teacher: How did the reporter put it together? What do you notice?

Student: He tells you about what happened and then gives an opinion on it.

Teacher: You're right. In the first paragraphs the writer tells what happened, and then later he gives his opinion. What information do you get from the first paragraphs, before he gives his opinion?

Student: He tells you what happened, who was there, and when it was.

Teacher: OK. You have pointed out a specific approach journalists usually use. They tell what happened, who was there, when it happened, where it happened, and why it happened. What, who, when, where, and why. Right?

Now look at your notes. What did you write that tells you what happened?

Student: Well, "the city council," that's who. "The meeting," that's what. "People wanted to get some help," that's why. I can put all that first. I'll say where the meeting was and how many people came. That's the basics.

Teacher: Great. Sounds like a good first paragraph to me. What's next?

Student: I could tell the details of what happened, like who spoke, and what they said, stuff like that.

Teacher: Excellent.

Student: Then at the end, I could put my opinion of what happened. I could say: "In my opinion . . ." so they know this isn't facts anymore.

Teacher: You've got it. Let me know when you have your draft.

Using Invented Spelling

In the drafting stage, the teacher shows a student a strategy for spelling that keeps the focus on writing for meaning rather than on correct spelling.

The Moment

Repeatedly hesitating over the spelling of words, a student is unable to concentrate on her ideas. The teacher shows her how to proceed so spelling is not a barrier to writing the first draft.

Student: How do you spell *nursing home?*

The Intervention

Teacher: What parts of it do you know?
Student: I'm not sure.
Teacher: What does *nursing* start with?
Student: An *n?*
Teacher: Sure. And what else do you hear in *nursing?*
Student: It ends in *-ing.*
Teacher: You're absolutely right. Write the parts of the word that you know. You can draw a line for the missing part if you want.
Student: So, I write *n——ing?*
Teacher: Yes. That's how to get the word down for now. We'll come back to it later. Read what you've written so far and then continue from there.
Student: How do you spell *elderly?*
Teacher: Don't worry about spelling. Do the best you can and move on.

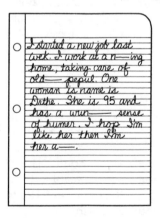

Teacher: Can you read it back to me?
Student: Sure. "I started a new job last week. I work at a nursing home taking care of old people." No, that's supposed to be *elderly* people. "One woman's name is Dorothy. She's 95 and has a wonderful sense of humor. I hope I'm like her when I'm her age."
Teacher: That's great. You were able to read the whole thing even though you weren't sure about how to spell some words. When you first write your ideas, it's important to let your thoughts flow freely. Don't worry about spelling. Spell as much of the word as you can and move on. Dorothy sounds like an interesting person. I'd like to hear more about her.

Expanding a First Draft

As a revision technique, the teacher shows a student how to incorporate into his writing the new things he says as he reads his writing aloud.

The Moment

As a student reads a first draft aloud in a writing conference, the teacher notices that he is adding to what he wrote as he reads it. She shows the student how to use the new things he's said to expand his story.

The Intervention

Teacher: I noticed that as you read, you added three things. You said the name of the city where you grew up. You said that your sisters came home dirty from head to toe, and you said that nobody knows if the money was ever claimed. Do you want to add these things to your story?

Student: That would be OK. How do I do that?

Teacher: Write down the points you added below the story. Number each point according to where it fits in the story. Go back to the story and write the number one where the first point goes, the number two where the second point goes, and the number three where the third point goes. When you rewrite, you can add each point in the place where you've put its number.

Student: That'll work.

Teacher: It's a good strategy for revising what you write. Read your draft to someone and take notes on any new information that you add. Then, when you rewrite, you can insert the new information.

Showing Not Telling

In the revision stage, the teacher points out the examples of vivid writing a student has produced and encourages her to continue to write this way.

The Moment

Teacher: So, Mary, this was your very first night in the shelter. I like how you show the people milling around and compare them to animals in the zoo. You paint a picture for the reader there. Also, when you describe the faces, you are showing us what you mean.

Student: Well, that's what they look like. I want the reader to see it.

The Intervention

Teacher: That's called showing. You are not just telling what happened, but you've described it so we can see the picture for ourselves. Showing is a lot more effective than telling. You do that very well. Are there other places in the story where you think you could show instead of tell?

Student: Here, where I say, "the smell is nauseating," I could say what the smells are and what they smell like, so people can smell it for themselves.

Teacher: I'm sure you will give us a sense of what the smells in the shelter were like. You are very good at showing. It's one of the things that makes your writing so effective.

Making Sense of Paragraphs

Sometimes a teachable moment about one stage of writing occurs while working on another. During the planning stage, a student asks a question about how to make paragraphs. Because writing is recursive, each stage involving the others, the teacher is able to discuss paragraphing in a way that helps the student plan what he wants to write.

The Moment

A student and teacher are conferring on possible topics for a GED essay when the student asks a question about how to construct a paragraph. Briefly, the teacher takes up this editing question. The examples he gives help the student think about paragraphing as a way to plan his writing.

Student: Well, one thing I could say is that TV is a big invention.

Teacher: Do you want that to be your essay topic or just a paragraph?

Student: I know this is a dumb question, but what is a paragraph? I mean, what goes in it?

The Intervention

Teacher: That's an editing question, and a very important one when you write the GED essay. What do you think makes a paragraph?

Student: When you have sentences together.

Teacher: Right, you can indent to show a paragraph, or you can put extra spacing between paragraphs. How do you decide which sentences go together?

Student: Well, you don't want too many sentences together. So every once in a while you make a paragraph.

Teacher: That's true. Paragraphs help make reading easier. But in a paragraph all the sentences are related by their ideas. For example, if you decide that you want to write an essay about TV, you can have a paragraph that talks about the ways TV is good and then another paragraph to talk about the ways TV is bad. If you think TV is more bad than good, you can have several paragraphs that tell the ways TV is bad. Each paragraph can describe one way TV is bad.

Student: Yeah. I know one way TV is bad. It makes you lazy.

Teacher: Let's say you make that the topic sentence. "TV makes you lazy." In the rest of the paragraph you can write how TV makes you lazy.

Student: You sit around, and half the time you don't know what you're watching. You don't go outside. You don't talk to people. You don't read.

Teacher: Right. All those ideas belong together in a paragraph. So do you want to write an essay on TV?

Student: Yeah. There's plenty I can say about TV. I can say something different about TV in each paragraph.

Teaching a Spelling Pattern

In the editing stage, the teacher helps a student improve her spelling by teaching a word pattern to overcome a repeated spelling error.

The Moment

Teacher: Read your writing to check if you are satisfied with what it says.

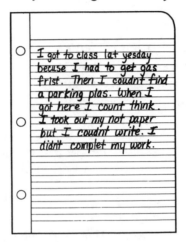

Student: "I got to class late yesterday because I had to get gas first. Then I couldn't find a parking place. When I got here I couldn't think. I took out my notebook paper, but I couldn't write. I didn't complete my work." It's OK. It's done.

The Intervention

Teacher: Now let's edit a few of the spelling errors. We'll focus on one type of error because there are a couple of places where it happens. Take a look at the following words in your story. Why don't you underline them as I say them: *late, place, note, complete.*

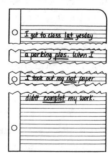

Teacher: OK. What word were you trying to write here? (He points to *lat.*)
Student: That's supposed to be *late.*
Teacher: Do you know how it would be pronounced as you've written it? What's another word that looks the same but has a different first letter?
Student: *Sat?*
Teacher: Exactly. So if *s-a-t* is *sat,* what would *l-a-t* be?
Student: *Lat?* But I wanted *late.*

Teacher: Good work. Being able to tell when a word is misspelled is the first step toward correcting it. That's called "proofreading." You need to be able to proof your work, read what's actually there, before you can make good changes. Let's see how you can proof the other words you underlined.

What word were you trying to write here? (He points to *plas.*)

Student: *Plas* is like *gas.* I want it to say *place. Not* is like *not home* or *not me.* I want it to say *note.* And *complet* is like *complex.* But I want it to say *complete.*

Teacher: OK. We know what the words you wrote say, and we know what you were trying to say. Now let's figure out how to spell them. Here, look at this list of words. Which of these words can you read?

write	hate
time	life
price	home

Student: "Write, time, piece."

Teacher: Try again with the last one.

Student: Oh, "Price. Price, hate, life, home."

Teacher: Great. And are the vowel sounds in these words short or long? Let's start with *life.*

Student: /L/ . . . /ī/ . . . /f/ That's long. The *i* says its name.

Teacher: Excellent. How about the others?

Student: They're all long vowels.

Teacher: Now, here are two lists of words that are slightly different from each other. Can you say how they are different?

tim	time
hat	hate
not	note

Student: Well, the words in the second column end in *e,* but you don't hear it.

Teacher: Yes, that's a big difference. How about the vowel sounds? How are they different?

Student: The words in the first list have short vowels, and in the second list, the vowels are long.

Teacher: You've got it! And what do you suppose is making the vowels long?

Student: Must be the *e.*

Teacher: Exactly. Words with a long vowel sound often end in silent *e.*

Student: So I need to add an *e* at the end of the underlined words so they sound right.

Using a Personal Speller

For poor spellers, a dictionary is not an efficient tool for finding out how words are spelled. As an alternative aid, a student can make a personal speller. A personal speller is an alphabetized list of words and accompanying sentences. The words are chosen by students because they use them and want to learn how to spell them correctly. Here, in the editing stage, a student gains experience using his personal speller.

The Moment

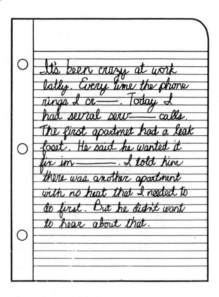

Teacher: Read what you wrote to make sure you are satisfied with it.
Student: "It's been crazy at work lately. Every time the phone rings I cringe. Today I had several service calls. The first apartment had a leaky faucet. He said he wanted it fixed immediately. I told him there was another apartment with no heat that I needed to do first. But he didn't want to hear about that." That's what I want to say.
Teacher: Which words do you have questions about?
Student: Well, I need to spell *cringe* and *immediately*.
Teacher: OK. Underline those and any others you'd like to check.

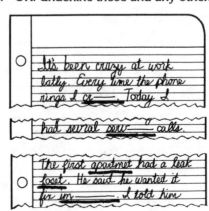

Teacher: What's one way you can find out the correct spellings?

Student: Some of these are in my personal speller. But I checked for *cringe*, and it isn't there.

Teacher: It has an odd spelling. Let me spell it for you, *c-r-i-n-g-e*. (The student fills it in.)

Student: But I've got *several*. I was pretty close, just one letter off.

Teacher: You did a lot better than the last time you tried to write it.

Student: I have *service*, too. I can't find *apartment*. What should I do with that one?

Teacher: Well, let's look at it again. Can you sound it out?

Student: "A . . . part . . . ment." Oh, I just left out a letter. I see.

Teacher: Actually, you spelled it correctly the second time you used it.

Student: I don't have *faucet* in my speller.

Teacher: It's spelled *f-a-u-c-e-t*.

Student: And *immediately?*

Teacher: *I-m-m-e-d-i-a-t-e-l-y*. You're making excellent progress. Did you notice that this time you could spell some of the words you put in your speller? And you're able to use your speller to look up words that you need.

Student: Well, thanks. But there are still some words I couldn't spell today. I guess I should add those to the list.

Teacher: Choose words that are most important for you, ones you are likely to use again in your writing.

Student: I think I want to add *faucet,* because I use it in my work. And *immediately* because it's so common and hard to spell!

Teacher: Good choices. Write in each word under its first letter. Then, write a sentence next to it to help you remember the meaning.

Pages from a Personal Speller:

S	
said	I said no!
should	I'm late. I should go.
several	I called him several times but got no answer.
special	My daughter's birthday was a special day.
second	First is 1. Second is 2.
strange	Ben had a strange look on his face because he was sad.
service	A good part of my day is spent on service calls.

T	
thought	I thought we were friends!
their	neighbor's yard = their yard
there	Look over there.
true	He's a true blue friend
trailer	I haul wood in my trailer.

CHAPTER 9 SPOKEN-LANGUAGE ACTIVITIES

Reading, writing, listening, and speaking are all related. Each aspect of language contributes to another. By speaking and listening we improve our ability to read and write. By reading and writing we improve our ability to speak and listen. Together, spoken- and written-language activities help adult learners increase their general knowledge of language and improve their communication skills.

Varied opportunities to communicate enhance our ability to understand and be understood. Through broad experience with spoken and written language, we expand our ability to communicate different types of messages for different purposes. Telling a story is similar to reading a story. Having a discussion is similar to writing an essay.

As teachers, we can interweave spoken and written language throughout instruction, making discussion and role plays part of reading and writing, and encouraging reading and note taking for speeches and presentations.

Students can be introduced to new vocabulary, phrases, or types of sentences in spoken-language activities, and then apply what they learn to reading and writing. Through speaking and hearing language in use, they can also feel more comfortable using different ways of expressing ideas and trying out words and phrases that they first encounter in print. Most adults feel at home in spoken language and appreciate the freedom these activities allow to explore language and communication.

This chapter describes spoken-language activities designed to create a personal language dictionary, act out situations, structure thinking in discussion, have a roundtable discussion, and make a speech.

Creating a Personal Language Dictionary

As students become aware of variations in language use, they may enjoy exploring terms and expressions they use in everyday speech. The topic of language variations may arise when students ask about how to speak in a job interview, or how to compare language used in a formal speech and a conversation, or talk about language use in different places or ethnic or cultural groups. If students are learning about dictionaries or have access to different types of dictionaries, such as a sports dictionary or a slang dictionary, they may want to create a personal language dictionary of the terms and expressions they use in their everyday speech.

Exploring their personal vocabularies is a way for students to establish ties between their everyday language and the formal language in most reading and writing. At first, students may hesitate to discuss language that is usually considered outside the bounds of a learning situation. Personal language may include sexual references and derogatory expressions, so be prepared to set boundaries if necessary.

Purpose: To validate students' personal expressions as legitimate and creative uses of language.

Materials: A flip chart or chalkboard, a computer (optional), and various dictionaries corresponding to students' reading levels (standard dictionaries, slang dictionaries, foreign-language dictionaries, and thesauruses).

Process:

> Talk about language variations
>
> Collect personal expressions
>
> Discuss what a dictionary is
>
> Make a dictionary

Talk about language variations

In response to students' comments or questions about the different ways people use language, ask students to think about their own language use.

> **Teacher:** We all have experience with using different kinds of language for different occasions. What are some differences in how we talk in our community, with friends, and on the job? Language changes over time. What are some expressions that you use and your parents don't, or that your parents use and you don't? Words come from different sources. Some words come from other languages. Some words are shortened versions of other words. Technology creates new words. Are there any words or expressions that you use whose origins you can identify?

Collect personal expressions

Invite students to consider their own varied use of language and to identify words and expressions they use for different occasions. Ask students to decide on a particular type of personal language to explore, and make lists of words and expressions. To begin the activity, the whole class can brainstorm a short list of slang or other informal expressions. To gather more words, students can interview each other in small groups and interview people outside class. Then students create lists of words and share them with the whole class. They review the words together and decide what additional information to provide for each word.

Teacher: We all have different types of language we speak in different situations. We use slang when we talk informally with our friends, regional expressions that are particular to the area of the country we live in, and expressions we use only within the family, on the job, and at school. Let's decide what type of language to explore. We can all work on the same type of language or choose different types. We may decide to use the lists to create a dictionary.

Discuss what a dictionary is

If students decide they want to create their own dictionary, lead a discussion to start students thinking about dictionaries as a collection of words for a particular type of language. Dictionaries represent a mainstream of language and are updated over the years. Words are added and removed to reflect changes in language use. New words reflect cultural shifts, new technology, new events, and new populations. Words and expressions may become acceptable once they are used by professional writers. There are many different kinds of dictionaries. For example, a baseball dictionary defines terms used in baseball.

Teacher: Why do we have dictionaries? Why are new dictionaries published every few years? Do the words change or stay the same? What does this reflect? Not all language is in a dictionary. Why? What are some different kinds of dictionaries?

Make a dictionary

Prepare the lists as entries in a dictionary. Ask students to decide which elements to include in their dictionaries. Basic elements include alphabetical order, single words or phrases, definitions, and example sentences. Other elements might be parts of speech and illustrations. Distribute the prepared lists to students. You can either end the activity at this point or have the class actually publish a dictionary by preparing the manuscript and designing the book. Once it is complete, celebrate and share the dictionary with others.

Sample: Creating a Personal Language Dictionary

Creating a Slang Dictionary

When their teacher brought in a slang dictionary produced by students in a literacy program in New York City, a mixed-level class of young adults from the inner city decided to create a dictionary of their own. The teacher was glad that they were finally willing to explore their own speech in class. In the year that they had been together, these students often used slang when they spoke to each other but, until now, they had been very reluctant to talk about their slang with the teacher. The project lasted five sessions.

Purpose: To help students produce a document to say, "this is who we are." To explore concepts of language differences and word origins, and to learn about dictionaries by creating one.

Talk about language variation and collect personal expressions

The teacher circulated the slang dictionary produced by students in another program and asked her students to see if the expressions differed from their own. She asked them to give examples of expressions they used, and they all agreed that she would list them on the board. Students offered so many examples that she soon ran out of space. She taped a number of flip chart pages on the walls and filled them.

Teacher: When I was in New York City, I picked up this dictionary called *Street Talk!** from a youth program there. I think their slang is different from yours.

Students: How? Let's see. What kind of slang do they have in New York City?

Teacher: In order to compare your slang to theirs, we need to see yours. Write down the slang you use, and then we can compare.

Student: I don't want to write it down. It's nasty.

Teacher: Write down what you are comfortable with. We'll talk about the nasty stuff later.

Student: No, how about if you write it on the board, and we'll tell you what to write.

Teacher: OK. Let's brainstorm. Say the slang word and what it means. Define it. I'll write on the board.

The class brainstormed as the teacher listed their ideas on the board.

Teacher: Is your slang the same or different from New York City slang?

Student: It's mostly different.

Teacher: Why do you think it's different?

Student: Seattle slang comes from L.A. and Oakland gangs.

Student: Look, they got *five-o*. We got that.

Student: Everybody knows *five-o*. It's from that TV show. Don't need to be no gang member to know *five-o* is police.

Student: It's a lot of bad words, like we got.

Teacher: I wonder if that's why slang is created, so no one knows what we're saying. We can say bad words, or other words, in a code that only we understand.

---

* *Street Talk! A Youth Dictionary by the Teens of Washington Houses Community Center,* Union Settlement Association, 1990-1991.

Student:	It's how we talk. It's how we understand each other.
Student:	It's how we know someone's cool.
Teacher:	That's why I use slang, to express who I am. When I first moved here I had to learn Seattle-talk. It is so different from New York.
Student:	In Virginia they use different words than here.
Student:	Can we do this too? Make a dictionary or something?
Teacher:	Sure. I'll type this list on the computer, and we'll go from there.

Discuss what a dictionary is and make a dictionary

In the next two sessions, students discussed their reasons for wanting to make a dictionary. To plan their own dictionary, they examined other dictionaries to decide which features they wanted to include in theirs. They chose alphabetical order, and the main parts of speech (noun, verb, adjective, adverb). They worked in pairs to write definitions and sample sentences for each word they chose from the list.

At the next two meetings the class finalized the alphabetical order of the word list and decided which part of speech each term was. The teacher suggested that they look at how they used the words in sentences and decide if they were used as a noun, verb, adjective, or adverb. Using a computer, the teacher typed the students' list of words and added information that the students provided: alphabetical order, parts of speech, definitions, and sample sentences. Students volunteered to help input the parts of speech and final alphabetical order. Pages for the dictionary were prepared and copies were given to each student, but the project ended before the dictionaries were made.

Student:	This is good. Making this dictionary so people understand our words—understand us.
Student:	Maybe we can send it to that place in New York?
Teacher:	Maybe we could. What do you want in this dictionary besides words and definitions?
Student:	We should have how it's used. How you say it right.
Teacher:	You could write some sentences to show how the words are used. Everybody write a sentence for each word you know. The whole group can vote on the sentences you like best for the dictionary.
Student:	Can we have more than one sentence?
Teacher:	Let's look in a dictionary and see how it's done.
Student:	Yeah. They got different sentences to use the word different ways.
Teacher:	What other things do you think we need to make these words into a dictionary?
Student:	Why don't we look at a dictionary and make it look like that?
Teacher:	OK. Let's work in small groups for this. We have four dictionaries, so we'll have four groups. Look at the way the words are organized and at the information the dictionary gives for each word. Decide what you want to use.
Students:	Alphabetical order and parts of speech. Definitions and sentences.

The students got a sense of accomplishment from participating in the project. They shared individual pages of the dictionary with friends in and out of class. They had made a rich and personal contribution to understanding language, its uses, variety, and history.

Slang Dictionary Pages:

A	
Audi	v. Leave Audi man, here comes five-c

B	
Back	n. Butt That girl has a lot of back in that dress.
Bailed	v. to leave I'm bailen up to the set.
Bird	n. Kilo of cocaine He got busted with a bird.
Bogus	adj. Bummer/sucks Man that story is bogus.
Boots	n. Woman I'll be knockin boots tonight.
Booty	n. Butt Shake your booty.
Bremo	adj. Fat That guy is bremo.
Buckled	adj. Ugly They was dissen that buckled hoe.

C	
Cave	n. Dark place to do it Let's swoop down to the cave.
Chicken George	n. Brothers who like white women I will never be a Chicken George because I like black women.
Chillin	v. Taking it easy We just be chillin tonight.
Clownin	v. Showing off Man, you be clownin.
C note	n. Hundred dollars I'm bouts ta go get a C note from my homie.

D	
Dank	n. Pot I got to have some dank.
Dis	v. Disrespect Hey, don't dis me.
Dope	adj. Good Dam look dope to me.
Droppin science	v. Giving knowledge Main source is droppin science.

Acting It Out: Improvisation and Role Play

Improvisations and role plays are ways to use dramatic acting to create and explore situations. They provide an added dimension for discussions, reading, and writing. They help students see different perspectives, discover new ideas, experiment with wording, and explore options.

Improvisation

This technique stimulates both imagination and spontaneity. Improvisations (improv) are relatively unstructured. They can be realistic or pure fantasy. Improvisations allow for some of the most open exploration and creativity that dramatic acting provides. An improvisation is an excellent activity to use whenever students need to release tension, have fun, and explore their own creativity.

The class brainstorms a list of possible situations and possible settings, then selects a situation and setting for the improv. The situation and setting can be congruent (eating lunch in a restaurant) or incongruent (talking to your boss in a tree house). Students volunteer to play the scene. The dialogue goes wherever they take it. The only constraint is that they each must be responsive to what the other person says. The other students are the audience. They cannot interrupt the improv, but at any time, any member of the audience can enter the scene and become a player. The improv lasts until the players end it. After the improv, the class discusses what they saw and gives their responses to it.

Purpose: To experience new possibilities by acting and observing a scene that requires quick and spontaneous interaction.

Materials: Chalkboard or flip chart, sufficient space to move around, chairs arranged in a semicircle.

Process:
- Suggest an improv
- State the rules
- Brainstorm situation and setting
- Do the scene
- Discuss the scene

Suggest an improv

Explain to students that an improv is a technique used by actors, musicians, and artists to loosen up and develop some fresh approaches. To develop versatility, actors are given a situation, and they take it wherever it goes.

> **Teacher:** Let's get a change of pace by doing an improv.

State the rules

Explain to students how to do an improvisation.

> **Teacher:** In an improv you have to go with the flow, no matter how unlikely the situation. The players build on whatever is said. The only rule is never say no. The players must act on all the information given

them. For example, if the other player says to you, "How're the kids?" that may be new information to you, but now you know you've got children. The audience can't interrupt to give suggestions during the improv, but anybody can join in as another player in the scene at any time. When the actors end the scene, we'll all discuss it.

Brainstorm situation and setting

Have students first brainstorm a list of possible situations, then a list of possible settings. Then, let them select one situation and one setting for the improv. Unlikely combinations are often the most effective. They signal to the students that this is an occasion to try out something new and different, to let go.

> **Teacher:** Let's brainstorm a list of situations. Then we can brainstorm a list of settings. Then we'll choose one situation and one setting for the improv.

Situations
confronting your boss
having a job interview
getting caught lying
meeting a guy

Settings
in a gym
in a tree house
on a TV show
on Mars

Do the scene and discuss the scene

After the class selects the situation and the setting, invite students to volunteer to play the scene. The students can choose their parts.

After the improv, thank the players and audience. Ask the players what was new to them, how they felt doing the improv, and what they thought about it. Ask the audience to share their reactions. Students can select another situation and setting and do another improv.

Role Play

A role play is more structured than an improv. Role plays often involve real-life situations. Players are assigned a role and told the purpose of the exchange. Role plays allow students to experience new roles and practice alternative approaches to problematic situations. This is a particularly helpful technique for students who are shy or who lack confidence, since it enables them to take risks in a supportive environment.

Purpose: To try out communication strategies for use in the real world.

Process:

> Set the purpose
>
> Ask for situations
>
> Set up the role play
>
> Do the role play
>
> Discuss the role play

Set the purpose

Suggest a role play as a demonstration or as a way to explore a topic.

> **Teacher:** We've been talking about problem solving as a win-win situation. We can do a role play as a trial run at reaching mutual agreement, negotiating for a positive outcome.

Ask for situations

Ask students to suggest places and situations that relate to the topic.

> **Teacher:** What are some situations in your lives that require negotiation?
> **Students:** Talking to my child's teacher. Getting the landlord to paint my apartment. Solving a problem at work.

Set up the role play

Work out a scenario and assign roles.

> **Student:** Let's do a role play on talking to the boss about some work that is late. The employee is worried about losing the job and needs to explain to the boss what happened. The boss doesn't want to fire the employee but needs to make sure that this problem doesn't happen again.
> **Teacher:** Sounds good. Divide into two groups. Each group can take one point of view. One group will decide what the issues are for the boss and what the boss might say; the other will do the same for the employee. We'll have one volunteer from each group do the role play.

Do the role play

The class watches students do a brief role play for 5–10 minutes. Here is a part of it:

Employee: I need to tell you about a problem I'm having. I'm very sorry about it.

Boss: What is it? We really can't afford any more things going wrong.

Employee: I'm late with the work. I've talked with the rest of the team, and we've got a new plan so this won't happen again.

Boss: You did the right thing. We'd better all meet together to find out what caused this problem to happen so we can avoid it in the future.

Discuss the role play

Ask players and audience to give feedback and share what they learned from the role play.

Teacher: OK. Let's give feedback about this interaction. Do you think the problem-solving strategies were effective?

Student: The employee took responsibility for the problem and had a plan of action to solve it. I like how he said "problem" and "I've got a plan" and "team." He knew the right words.

Student: And the boss did a good job, too. She got involved. That's good to be up front like that. And she said something nice to the worker to let him feel a little better and not worry that he would lose his job.

Structuring Thinking in a Discussion

During discussions students express ideas and make connections among them. This technique* helps students organize their ideas for reading, writing, and working on theme projects. Students brainstorm ideas, cluster them, label the clusters, and make statements about the overall relationships among the ideas.

Purpose: To enable students to explore and relate ideas in a discussion.

Materials: Chalkboard or flip chart.

Process:
> Focus on a topic

> Brainstorm

> Organize responses into clusters

> Make statements to connect the clusters

> Tie discussion to the larger activity

Focus on a topic

Remind students of the topic that they are currently pursuing, and set a purpose for the discussion.

> **Teacher:**   As we get ready to deal with the issue of women and work, let's discuss what you already know about the topic.

Brainstorm

Ask students to name everything they can think of that is related to the topic. Write their responses in a list on the board.

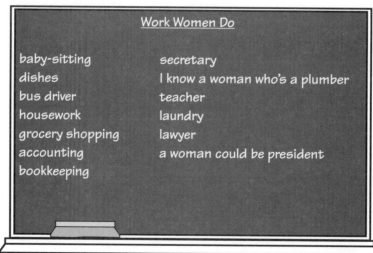

> Work Women Do
>
> baby-sitting   secretary
> dishes   I know a woman who's a plumber
> bus driver   teacher
> housework   laundry
> grocery shopping   lawyer
> accounting   a woman could be president
> bookkeeping

---

* From *Teacher's Handbook for Elementary Social Studies,* by H. Taba, Addison-Wesley, 1967.

Organize responses into clusters

Have students group responses that are related. Put the items in the clusters that the students suggest. Ask students to name each cluster by telling the reason for grouping the items. Then, write the name of the cluster above it. Items from the list may be used more than once or not at all.

Teacher: Which of these kinds of work can we put together because they are alike in some way?

Student: Dishes and laundry go together. They're housework.

Student: Baby-sitting fits there, too.

Student: Well, I don't think so. I think it's work.

Work Women Do			
Housework	Office work	College jobs	Other
dishes	bookkeeping	teacher	plumber
laundry	secretary	lawyer	president of USA
grocery	accounting	accounting	baby-sitting
shopping			bus driver

Make statements to connect the clusters

Ask students to make statements that include all of the clusters and individual ideas. If students need to explore relationships among clusters, they can make a mind map by putting each cluster in a circle and showing how the circles are connected to each other.

Teacher: What general statement could we make that would include all the things we've been talking about? What makes all these ideas make sense together?

Student: Women today have many more opportunities to work than they did in the old days.

Student: Women are doing more different jobs than they did before.

Student: Even though women can do more things today, we still have to do the housework.

Tie discussion to the larger activity

Suggest to students how to use the information as they proceed with the reading, writing, or theme project they are engaged in. After a prereading discussion, suggest that students read the selection to see if the author shares their views. After reading and discussing the ideas gained from reading, you may suggest that students write a paragraph stating what they think about the topic, using one of the general statements as their topic sentence. After discussing ideas for a theme project, suggest that students decide what to do next.

Having Roundtable Discussions

A roundtable discussion is a formal conversation to explore an issue or solve a problem. A discussion may span several sessions. In roundtable discussions, students develop language and communication skills, learn how to participate in a formal group, share their concerns, and plan actions.

This is an activity to introduce students to roundtable discussions. If you, instead of the students, choose the topic, be wary of volatile subjects that may cause friction within the group. As students get to know each other better and become familiar with roundtable discussions, let them take the lead in deciding on productive directions for the discussion.

Purpose: To have a productive group conversation.

Materials: A variety of reading material related to the issue, flip chart or chalkboard, a VCR and videotapes of TV debates and discussions (optional).

Process:

> Introduce the activity

> Set topic and purpose

> Facilitate the discussion

> Close the discussion

Introduce the activity

You may want to demonstrate a roundtable discussion by using tapes of TV programs in which experts with different points of view discuss an issue. Students who are on community boards or planning committees, or who work in teams on the job, can explain what happens in a formal planning or problem-solving discussion.

Teacher: A discussion is just two or more people sharing what they know about a topic, giving their opinions, and telling why they have those opinions. Sometimes we say people "argue" their sides. That doesn't mean they fight. They just try to convince others to agree with them. A roundtable discussion allows for give and take. We can change or modify our opinions a little or a lot as we work through the issues, and we can have a good time. We are interested in what others have to say, and they in turn are interested in our ideas.

Have you seen TV shows where a group of guests discuss government spending, health care, or family issues? The participants give their opinions and recommendations and tell why they have those ideas. Sometimes new ideas and plans grow out of these discussions.

Set topic and purpose

The topic should be of interest or concern to students. A good topic is one about which people can have differing opinions. Often a topic arises from what students have been reading, hearing about in the news, or talking about in the community. Frame the topic as a question. What is happening to "the family" today? What needs to be done to make the schools better? Also, identify the purpose of the discussion.

Teacher: What do we want to accomplish with this discussion? What outcome do we expect? Are we exploring a topic? Sharing information? Solving a problem? Reaching a decision or planning a course of action?

Facilitate the discussion

Help stimulate conversation. Invite students to share their ideas. Encourage them to ask each other questions, respond to what others have said, argue logically, and develop their argument. Help students appreciate the way they keep the group going as they ask how people are feeling, lighten tense moments with a joke, help the group get back on track, give others a chance to talk, and contribute by doing their share of talking.

You may also want to establish ground rules for discussions.

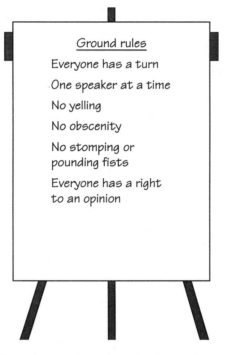

Ground rules

Everyone has a turn

One speaker at a time

No yelling

No obscenity

No stomping or pounding fists

Everyone has a right to an opinion

Chart the progress of the discussion. At intervals, have the group summarize what has been said and what still needs to be done. You may want to make a simple chart to show important parts that need to be covered. For problem solving, decision making, or planning you could make the following charts and use them to guide the discussion.

Teacher: Our purpose is to solve the problem. We've got a lot of information on the problem, but we can't solve it unless we figure out what caused the problem.

Problem-Solving Chart		
Problem	Cause	Solution

Teacher: Our purpose is to reach a decision. We know what we want to do, but how should we go about it?

Decision-Making Chart		
Options	Decisions	Implementation

Teacher: Our purpose is to plan. We're not clear yet about what our needs are.

Planning Chart		
Needs	Goals	Implementation

Close the discussion

Praise students for their accomplishment and, as a group, decide which steps to take next.

Teacher: This has been a very interesting discussion. You're getting experience in talking in front of others, trying out new ways of speaking, and getting your points across. And you know, a formal written essay is nothing but an argument on paper. So, after this, writing one will be easier, too.

Sample: Having Roundtable Discussions

Having a Problem-Solving Discussion

Parents who were participants in a family literacy program met twice a month for two-hour roundtable discussions related to their children's education. The teacher helped the group develop a rapport and become confident that they had valuable ideas to share. At this meeting, parents were upset about the rise of violence in their neighborhood. Putting aside the planned topic, the teacher suggested that they have a discussion to consider ways to solve the problem.

Purpose: To use discussion to deal with a real-life problem. To rehearse ways to articulate concerns to public officials.

Set topic and clarify purpose

The teacher helped the students identify a manageable topic.

Teacher: You're upset about the violence in the neighborhood. What is it that most concerns you?

Student: Every night people are shooting at each other in the streets.

Student: I'm afraid somebody's going to shoot my kids. I keep my whole family in the house like a bunch of prisoners. I'm afraid my kids will think this is normal.

Teacher: I'm hearing you say that you fear for your families because of this sudden increase in violence in the community. We have used our discussion times together as ways of addressing problems. So let's look at this as a problem and see what we can do about it. Let's focus on defining the problem, the causes for the problem, and possible solutions that will deal with the causes. Then we can decide which solutions we will attempt.

Facilitate the discussion

The teacher asked questions and summarized information to help the discussion progress. The teacher helped the participants explore ideas related to the problem, its causes, and possible solutions.

Teacher: What is the specific problem we're dealing with? Let's explore the causes. Different people have different views on the causes of this problem. There are a lot of people to blame here—the drug dealers, people in the neighborhood, and the police. But who is actually doing the shooting?

Let's explore solutions. Does anybody want to offer a solution? Are we just talking pie-in-the-sky with these ideas, or is there something we can really do?

Throughout the discussion, the teacher encouraged students to use problem-solving terms to help get their points across. They used words such as *opinion, option, problem, cause,* and *solution.* As needed, he put sentence starters on the board.

Teacher: When you talk about what's causing the situation, you might want to start this way:

One cause is . . .

Teacher: What are possible ways of solving this problem? Try this out as you discuss the options:

One cause is . . .
One option is . . .
Another option is . . .

At this point the group had explored the various aspects of the situation but hadn't been able to come to a resolution. The teacher sketched a problem-solving chart on the board and asked the group to summarize the points so far. This process helped students renew their focus and move toward action.

Teacher: How far have we gotten? Let's summarize using this chart.

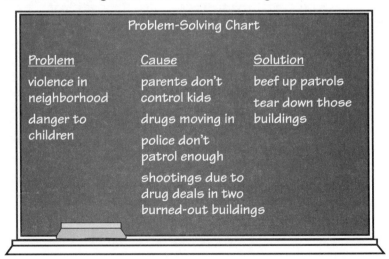

Problem-Solving Chart

Problem	Cause	Solution
violence in neighborhood	parents don't control kids	beef up patrols
danger to children	drugs moving in	tear down those buildings
	police don't patrol enough	
	shootings due to drug deals in two burned-out buildings	

Teacher:	So how do we let the appropriate people know what needs to be done to solve this problem?
Student:	We could write letters. We're all taxpayers.
Student:	No. That's too complicated. They need to look at us face-to-face.
Teacher:	Who's *they?*
Student:	The mayor. The police chief. The city council.
Student:	Let's meet them right here at the school. We'll all march down the hill and let them see those buildings.
Student:	I wish someone would tell me how we're going to get the mayor and all these other folks to come to our next meeting.
Teacher:	Good point. We need to make assignments. Who wants to call downtown and set up the meeting? Who wants to moderate the meeting? Who wants to do the talking?

Close the discussion

The teacher asked the group to evaluate the discussion.

Teacher:	Well, let's reflect on what we've done tonight. Finish these sentence starters:

Tonight I . . .
I wish . . .

Student:	Tonight I feel like we might have a shot at getting those buildings torn down.
Student:	Tonight I am very nervous thinking about talking to politicians.
Student:	Tonight I hope I sleep better.

Note: This dialogue actually happened. A representative from the mayor's office, the city council, and the police met with the group and 30 neighborhood residents whom the parents had invited. After planning and practicing, one parent made the presentation and another was the moderator for the discussion that followed. The buildings were torn down. Police patrols increased. The neighborhood became safer again.

Making a Speech

In this activity, students prepare and present a formal speech. In a formal speech, you combine spoken and written language. Students produce a complete text for an audience of more than one person. Even when the actual speech is not written out, planning, organizing, and polishing a speech parallel the stages of the writing process. The parts of a speech—introduction, argument, and conclusion—parallel the structure of reports and essays. Students can prepare speeches for actual occasions or as role plays. Because this activity has several distinct phases and may last for several sessions, you may want to provide students with a checklist to use as a guide. (See the Guide to Making a Winning Speech on page 149.)

Purpose: To engage students in preparing and presenting a speech.

Materials: A variety of reading materials for researching a topic, a VCR and videotapes of famous speeches (optional), audiotape or videotape recording equipment (optional).

Process:

> Select a topic and purpose
>
> Prepare the speech
>
> Practice the speech
>
> Deliver the speech
>
> Critique the speech

Select a topic and purpose

Students can prepare and present formal speeches for class or program-wide events. They can practice speeches for delivery to outside organizations, such as churches or clubs, or present their views on an issue for a formal classroom debate, and make speeches as role plays. Students can role-play while they deliver speeches. They can role-play authors whose work they've read, or people they've read about. They can role-play politicians, celebrities, or experts in a field.

> **Teacher:** Let's say you were the president. Prepare and give a speech to the nation on an important issue, or defend an action that you have taken. Lay out your views and try to persuade the audience to agree with you. We'll tape the speeches so you can see yourself in action.

Prepare the speech

Help students discuss and research their ideas.

> **Teacher:** Work together in small groups to decide on the ideas for your speech. By sharing your ideas, you act as sounding boards, helping each other sort out your reasoning. Through questioning, arguing, and giving suggestions you can each identify your topic and your opinions. You can select the supporting information—the facts, examples, expert advice, or other reasons—that you will use to help convince others of your opinion.

After students have planned the content, introduce a format for a persuasive speech and information to put in each part.

A format for a persuasive speech:

1. Introduction: Introduce yourself and your topic to the audience. You might tell a story that sets up the topic, or begin with a startling fact. You want to get the audience's attention and give a general idea of what you will be talking about.

2. Opinion statement: Say what you think about the topic. You want the audience to know your stand.

3. Supporting points: Give from two to four points to support your opinion. Organize your points so they have the greatest impact. You might start with your most important point first or leave it to the end. Use transition words or phrases to help the audience understand as you move from one supporting point to the next. You can say, "In the first place, . . . In the second place, . . . Finally, . . . and Most importantly, . . ." To let the audience know that you are going to give a reason, you might say, "The reason for this is . . ." To let the audience know you are going to give an example, you might say, "An excellent example is . . ." Think of words or phrases that give your audience clues to the kind of information you are providing.

4. Statement of opposing view: A good argument must address the other side of the issue. You don't have to go into detail about the other side. Just give the opposing view and follow it right away with more support for your view. Speakers often say things like, "I know there are those who believe that (give the opposing view). To them I say (support your view)." Another way to do this is to say, "Of course you may argue that (give the opposing view), but I would remind you that (give your view)."

5. Conclusion: Summarize or repeat your main point and clinch your argument with an interesting thought. The clincher should stick in your audience's mind long after the speech is over.

Practice the speech

Students should rehearse the speech aloud. They can do this at home in front of the mirror and in class. Students can revise the content, rehearse their delivery, and make sure that the speech fits within the set time limits.

Deliver the speech

Presenting the speech is an event. Treat the presentation as a special occasion for both audience and speakers.

Critique the speech

In role plays and other in-class situations, allow for a review of the speech as a learning experience for both the audience and speaker. A critique always mentions the good along with the bad. Reviewers should confirm the hard work that went into preparation of the speech and highlight positive aspects of the content and delivery. An audience feedback sheet can help keep the focus on salient points. (See the Audience Feedback Checklist on page 150.)

Guide to Making a Winning Speech

Directions: Consider these questions as you prepare and critique your speech.

Preparation

Gathering Ideas

What is the topic?

What do I think or feel about the topic?

Why do I have this view?

What research should I do?

Who should I share my ideas with?

Composing the Speech

How will I organize my ideas?

How will I get the audience to agree with me?

Beginning

How do I introduce myself?

How do I introduce the topic?

How do I introduce my opinion?

How do I shift to the body of the speech?

Middle

What are my supporting points?

What type of reasons do I give?

How do I explain each point?

How do the points fit together?

How do I address the opposing view?

End

How do I end the speech?

What is my clincher?

Practicing the Speech

Where should I rehearse the speech aloud?

Is the speech the right length?

What changes should I make?

How is my delivery?

Presentation

What did I plan that worked well?

What worked well that I did not plan?

What didn't work so well?

Critique

How do I think I did?

What does the audience think?

What have I learned?

What will I keep in mind for next time?

Audience Feedback Checklist

Reviewer _____   Speaker _____

Topic of Speech _____   Date _____

Yes   No

Presentation

____ ____ Did the speech have an introduction?

____ ____ Could I tell what the topic was?

____ ____ Could I tell the speaker's opinion?

____ ____ Could I tell why the speaker had this view?

____ ____ Did the speech seem well organized?

____ ____ Were there details to make the ideas clear?

____ ____ Did the speaker admit there are other points of view?

____ ____ Did the speaker end the speech effectively?

____ ____ Did the speaker do a good job trying to win me over?

Preparation

____ ____ Did the speaker know the topic?

____ ____ Was the information interesting?

____ ____ Did the speaker say where the information came from?

Delivery

____ ____ Was the speaker loud enough?

____ ____ Did the speaker talk at a good speed?

____ ____ Did the speaker make eye contact with the audience?

____ ____ Did the speaker's voice vary to keep my interest?

____ ____ Was the speech a good length?

Overall, I think the speech was: _____

_____.

Overall, I think the speaker's presentation was: _____

_____.

Helpful things I can tell the speaker are: _____

_____.

CHAPTER 10 TEACHING SKILLS IN MINI-LESSONS

What is a mini-lesson?

A mini-lesson is a stand-alone period of between 5 and 30 minutes for direct instruction of a skill or any instructional element. It is a self-contained activity that focuses on an element of reading and writing that students need to learn. A brief mini-lesson in each session gives you and your students a planned way to pause and attend to a discrete and limited aspect of the reading and writing experience.

Most useful skills or discrete aspects of instruction can be taught in mini-lessons. A mini-lesson is a concentrated way to teach skills efficiently so you can devote most of the session to the broader activities that are the main business of instruction: engaging students in reading, writing, and discussion in order to understand and communicate important ideas and experiences.

Mini-lessons are most effective when students want to learn a particular skill to accomplish their current work or meet an important goal. To involve students in choosing what to teach in a mini-lesson, you can keep a list of skills you have noticed students need help with and ask them to choose from the list. You can also ask students what they need to complete a reading or writing activity. For example, as a student reaches the editing phase in a piece of writing, ask what kinds of corrections she wants to be able to make. Through conversation you can help students identify what they need to know to successfully complete a project or do an upcoming activity.

Steps in Teaching a Skill

- Teach

    Assess—Find out what the students already know about the subject.

    Explain—Tell the students what is going to be taught and why.

    Model—Show the students how to do it.

    Teach—Teach the skill or strategy.

- Practice

    Guided practice—Create situations or exercises that lead students to produce the desired behavior or response.

    Independent practice—Students practice with only a little assistance from you.

    Assess—Are students ready for the next step? If they are not, reteach.

- Apply

    Students use the new skill in their activities with little or no teacher involvement.

To teach a skill, investigate what students already know. Ask students to complete examples and explain the rules or procedures they used. This will allow you to address errors or misconceptions that students may have acquired in previous learning. When you teach, you pass on information by explaining what you will be teaching, by modeling, and by telling students how, when, and why they will need to use the skill.

Helping students reinvent or discover information for themselves is a powerful technique to use in a mini-lesson. A simple way to use the discovery method is to provide students with several correct examples of a skill or instructional element. Ask students to examine the examples together and discover the underlying rules or procedures.

Opportunity for practice is essential. Plenty of practice means the difference between temporary memorization and real learning. As students gain more mastery, they need less and less teacher intervention. Plan for practice in stages. For example, you can use whole-group instruction to expose students to correct responses, small-group practice to provide support from teacher and peers, and individual practice for students to reach independence.

After students have achieved some proficiency, encourage them to apply the skill on an ongoing basis in regular activities. At this stage, the teacher is available as a consultant, but the student is in charge.

This chapter contains mini-lessons on phonics practice, sound discrimination, word patterns, syllabication, sight words, vocabulary building, main idea and details, comparison and contrast, cause and effect, learning-style preferences, and study skills.

Practicing Phonics

Phonics instruction emphasizes the sound-letter correspondences in English words. In this activity, students practice saying sounds of letters they see, and writing letters for sounds they hear. Students practice only those sounds and letters that they know but have not yet mastered to the point of automatic recognition. The activity has two parts: a visual drill in which the students read letters on cards, followed by an auditory drill in which the students write letters from dictated sounds. Together the drills should take about 15 minutes. Students can work in pairs, small groups, or with a teacher.

Purpose: To practice and review common sound-letter relationships for reading and spelling.

Materials: Index cards.

Process:

- Assess each student's phonics base
- Each student makes a phonics card pack
- Demonstrate how to do the visual drill
- Students practice the visual drill
- Demonstrate how to do the auditory drill
- Students practice the auditory drill
- Add new cards

Assess each student's phonics base

To determine which phonic elements each student knows well enough to practice and review, use a phonics checklist. (See the Phonics Checklist on page 157.) Ask the student to say the sound each letter stands for. If he cannot say it immediately, suggest that he think of a word containing the letter. Be careful not to give him too much help. The assessment should indicate which sound-letter combinations the student knows well, which ones he knows somewhat, and which ones he does not know at all.

Each student makes a phonics card pack

Have students make letter cards for each sound that they know either well or somewhat. They should not make cards for sounds that they do not recognize at all. Each learner will have a card pack. Each set of cards will be different, since each student recognizes a different set of letters.

To make the cards, students write the letter or letter group on one side of the card. On the other side of the card, the teacher or student writes a key word containing the letter(s). It must be a word that helps the student say and remember the sound for the letter(s). Students should decide what key word they want. If the sound can appear at the beginning of words, have a student choose a key word that starts with the sound. For example, *apple* is a better choice than *hat* for /a/.

| a | apple |

Demonstrate how to do the visual drill

Show students how to go through the pack. If the student says a sound easily, lay the card aside. If the student has difficulty, prompt the student with the key word and then have the student write the letter(s) and say the sound several times. Place the cards that are difficult back in the middle of the card pack.

Teacher: I am going to show you a way to practice recognizing written sounds so you will recognize them more easily when reading or writing. First, I'll show you how to do the visual drill. To demonstrate, I'll use one student's card pack. I will show you the cards one at a time. You say the sound for the letter(s) on the card. If you say the sound quickly without thinking, I'll lay the card aside and go on to the next card. If you have difficulty, I'll prompt you and let you practice. Then we'll put the card back in the pack so you can review it. Let's try.

The teacher and student work through the card pack.

Teacher: What sound does this make?
Student: I don't quite remember.
Teacher: It's like in your key word, *phone*. What sound do you hear at the beginning of *phone?*
Student: /f/.
Teacher: To help you connect the sound with the letters, write the letters *ph* a few times and each time you write, say the sound /f/. Then I'll put the card back in the card pack so you can review some more.

Continue showing cards one at a time. If a student knows more than one sound for the letter or letter group, there should be key words on the back of the card for each sound. Remind the student to say all the sounds he knows for the letter(s).

```
┌─────────────┐          ┌─────────────┐
│             │          │             │
├─────────────┤          │    cat      │
│             │          │    city     │
│      c      │          │             │
│             │          │             │
└─────────────┘          └─────────────┘
```

Student: /k/
Teacher: That's right. You know another sound, too.
Student: /s/
Teacher: Good.

Continue in this way, showing letters and asking for their sounds, until you have gone through the entire card pack one time. Then, go through the card pack several more times. With each round, the active pile should get smaller. You'll set more cards aside as the student recognizes more letter-sound relationships quickly.

Students practice the visual drill

Have students do the visual drill with each other. When two students work together, one takes the role of teacher. She will drill the other student using his cards and prompting him with his key words. The point of the drill is to attain instant recognition of letter-sound relationships, so the "teacher" needs to flip the cards quickly. Remind students to keep paper and pencil nearby so they can write down the sounds that give them trouble. When the first student has finished, the students exchange roles.

Demonstrate how to do the auditory drill

The auditory drill follows the visual drill. In the auditory drill, the teacher says sounds of letters in the student's card pack and the student writes the letters that spell the sounds. This drill is harder to do, so instead of using the whole card pack, choose only 8–10 cards to work with. Use a mix of easy and challenging cards. Say only the sounds for the letters. Do not use a whole word unless the student is stuck. If the student gets stuck, provide the key word as a memory aid. If the student then writes the target letter(s), go on to the next card. If the key word does not help, show the card and repeat the sound.

> **Teacher:** Now I'm going to show you how to practice writing letters for sounds you hear. I'll dictate a sound to you, and you write the letter or letters for that sound. Before you write, say the sound aloud to make sure you heard it right. If you know more than one way to write the sound, write it each way that you know.

The teacher and student begin the drill. After they have done a number of cards, the student writes down the wrong letter.

> **Teacher:** What letter did you write for /v/?

Student: Oh, I wrote *d*.

Teacher: Yes, but you want to write the letter for the sound /v/ like in your key word *victim*.

Student: Is this it?

Teacher: Here, look at the card and say the sound /v/ in *victim*. Write the letter *v* and say the sound a few times to help you remember it.

Students practice the auditory drill

After students have learned the procedure for the auditory drill, they can do the entire mini-lesson, first the visual drill, then the auditory drill, working in pairs.

Add new cards

As new sounds are introduced during other lessons and activities, students can make new cards to add to their pack. Students can take their card packs home and review them. Their phonics checklist can be updated to include new phonics elements as students learn them.

Note: Although progress can be measured using a phonics checklist, the best measure is how well these skills transfer to new reading and writing situations. As learners approach unfamiliar words in reading, refer them to their key words as clues in figuring out how to read the unfamiliar word. As they struggle to spell words, ask them about the sounds. Ask them which ways those sounds can be spelled. Encourage them to experiment. The more they learn about phonics, the more choices they will have.

Phonics Checklist

This checklist includes the most common phonetic elements in English. You can use this list to keep track of your progress in learning sound-letter relationships.

Directions:

Check (✓) the letters whose sounds you know automatically (without thinking).

Circle the letters you are learning but don't know completely.

To help yourself, you can read the sample word next to the letter(s) and then say the sound of the letter(s).

When you have learned the sound for a letter, place a check mark (✓) next to it.

Don't mark any letter whose sound you don't know at all.

Consonants

				Short Vowels
__b (bat)	__j (jam)	__qu (quit)	__x (tax)	__a (at)
__c (car)	__k (kiss)	__r (run)	__y (yes)	__e (Ed)
__d (dog)	__l (lake)	__s (sun)	__z (zoo)	__i (it)
__f (fun)	__m (moon)	__t (take)		__o (on)
__g (go)	__n (no)	__v (van)		__u (up)
__h (happy)	__p (pill)	__w (water)		

Digraphs   Second Consonant Sounds   R-controlled Vowels

Digraphs	Second Consonant Sounds	R-controlled Vowels
__sh (she)	__c (city)	__er (her)
__ch (chair)	__g (gin)	__ar (car)
__th (thin)	__s (is)	__or (corn)
__th (then)		__ir (bird)
__wh (when)		__ur (fur)
__ph (phone)		

Silent-*e* Syllables   Open Syllables   Vowel Pairs

Silent-*e* Syllables	Open Syllables	Vowel Pairs	
__ate (date)	__a (ba/con)	__ee (see)	__ea (eat)
__ete (Pete)	__e (me)	__oa (boat)	__ea (head)
__ife (life)	__i (pi/lot)	__ay (day)	__oo (food)
__ome (home)	__o (o/pen)	__ai (wait)	__oo (book)
__ute (cute)	__u (hu/man)	__oy (boy)	__ow (slow)
__ype (type)	__y (cry)	__oi (coin)	__ow (cow)
__y (ba/by)	__aw (saw)		

Practicing Sound Discrimination

In this activity, students practice discriminating between similar sounds that they have previously confused or used interchangeably. Students can practice either visual discrimination for reading or auditory discrimination for spelling. Either type of activity should take about 10 minutes. Prepare short lists of word pairs that contain the pairs of sounds students need to practice. For reading, students read the lists. For spelling, students write the words as you dictate them. The activity can be repeated over several sessions.

Some types of common sound discrimination problems are:

Short vowel discrimination (*pit/pet; nut/not; bad/bed*)

Beginning or ending consonant discrimination (*tip/dip; cab/cap*)

Single consonant and consonant blend discrimination (*bag/brag*)

Short vowel/long vowel discrimination (*fat/fate; fit/feet*)

Purpose: To provide practice in discriminating between similar sounds for either reading or spelling.

Materials: Short lists of word pairs.

Process:

Introduce the mini-lesson for reading

Use lists for modeling and practice

Students read other words

Introduce the mini-lesson for spelling

Use lists for modeling and practice

Students spell other words

Introduce the mini-lesson for reading

Teacher: I've noticed that you've been confusing two short vowel sounds when you read. This activity will help you learn the difference between them so you won't get them mixed up when you read.

Use lists for modeling and practice

Make two short lists. Label each list with one of the target sounds and the student's key word for that sound. In each list, put in simple words containing the target sound. In a few rows, include pairs of words that differ only in the feature students need to discriminate (minimal pairs). For example, to help students practice discriminating between the short vowel sounds /a/ and /e/, you can use word pairs like *sat* and *set*.

```
  a        e

apple    Ed

sat      set

bat      bet

lag      leg

pat      pet
```

First, model reading. As a warm-up, read all the words in one list. Then, read all the words in the other list. Say each word. Repeat the word, drawing out the target sound. Then, say the sound in isolation. Then, say the word again. You can ask the student to read each list after you. Finally, read the pairs of words in each row. Point to each word as you read. Ask the student to read after you.

> **Teacher:** Now that we have read the list of words that have the sound /a/ as in your key word *apple,* and the list of words that have the sound /e/ as in *Ed,* let's read across the rows so you can tell the difference between the words. I'll read first; then, you read after me. We'll read across the rows like this: "Sat . . . s-a-t . . . /a/ . . . sat. Set . . . s-e-t . . . /e/ . . . set. Sat/set. . . . Set/sat."

After you have read down both lists and have shown the student how to read one pair of words, the student is ready to practice the words. Read rows of word pairs randomly to lessen reliance on visual memory. Ask the student to point to each word you read. Then, ask the student to read the words out of order, pointing to each word as he reads. If the student makes an error, repeat the word and the sound in isolation, and use the key word to reinforce the sound.

> **Teacher:** Now I'll read the words to you. You point to each word I read. "Sat/pet, leg/bat, set/sat, bat/bet." Now, you read the words and point to each word as you read. Remember, first read a word in one list. Then, in the other list.

Students read other words

Ask the student to read other words that have the target sounds. Again, mix the list to lessen reliance on visual memory.

Introduce the mini-lesson for spelling

> **Teacher:** I've noticed that you haven't been distinguishing between two short vowels when you spell. This activity will help you hear the short vowel sounds better, so you won't mix them up when you spell.

Use lists for modeling and practice

Prepare two lists of words similar to those used for sound discrimination in reading. For spelling, it is not necessary for the word pairs to differ only in the target sound. The words do need to be simple and phonetically regular, however, since the focus is on sound discrimination. Don't show the student the list of words. Instead, draw two empty columns on a piece of paper. Write the target sounds and the key words for the sounds as headings.

To model the activity, point to each column, and say the key word and the target sound for each column. Reading from your prepared lists, present one word for each column. Say the word; repeat the word, drawing out the target sound; say the sound in isolation; and say the word again. Then, write the word in its column. Do the same with a word from the other column. Then, dictate the remaining words to the student, alternating a word from column one with a word from column two.

Teacher: I'll do the first pair of words to show you how. I say the word *sat*. Then I repeat the word slowly, *s-a-t*. I say the short vowel sound /a/. Then I say the word again, *sat*. Then I write the word in the /a/ column. Next I do the same with the word *pet*. Now I'll dictate other words for you to say. Sound them out, identify the short vowel sound, and write them.

<u>a</u>	<u>e</u>
apple	Ed
sat	pet
fan	bed
bad	leg
~~lamp~~ lap	end
trap	~~past~~ pest

If the student confuses the target sound, guide him by saying the appropriate key word. If he makes errors in other parts of the word, help him by sounding out the word. After the student has correctly spelled the words, ask him to read the words in both lists.

Students spell other words

Without using the columns as prompts, dictate additional words with the target sounds for the student to spell.

Note: It is not realistic to ask students to practice sound discriminations that don't exist in their dialects. If the student pronounces *pin* and *pen* the same way, then this exercise is not useful. Such pairs of words will need to be treated as homonyms in the learner's vocabulary. Spelling distinctions will need to be made using different means, such as learning these words as sight words and using them in context.

Teaching Word Families for Spelling

Word families are common patterns comprised of a vowel sound followed by one or more consonants such as *ack* or *ut*. Each word within a word family rhymes with the other words in that family and shares the same key spelling pattern (*back, track, tack; but, cut, rut*). This mini-lesson focuses on one or several related word patterns. The lesson includes both visual practice (remembering what the patterns look like) and auditory practice (being able to hear patterns within words).

Purpose: To help students improve their spelling by recognizing key word patterns rather than relying solely on remembering the letters in each word.

Materials: A fill-in-the-blank word exercise and sentence exercise.

Process:

Choose the word pattern
Build words for reading
Spell by sound substitution
Spell whole words
Spell words in sentences
Teach complementary word patterns

Choose the word pattern

It is most effective to teach spelling based on an observed need in students' writing. In this mini-lesson, the teacher chose the *-ill* pattern because a student had misspelled *fill* and *still* in a recent piece of writing.

Build words for reading

Ask the student to read a very simple word with the pattern. (Occasionally, the pattern itself is a word.) Then, ask the student to read other simple words with the pattern, isolate the pattern, and contribute other words that have the pattern. Then, read the words in random order to the student. Finally, ask the student to read the words.

Teacher: What is this word?

ill

Student: "Ill."
Teacher: Right. Now, read this list of words.

ill
hill
fill
still
mill

Teacher:	What's the same in all these words?
Student:	They all end the same.
Teacher:	Yes, they all end in -*ill*. Underline *ill* in each word. Let's add a few more words to this list. What other words rhyme with these words?
Student:	*Bill* and *kill*.
Teacher:	OK. I'll add those words to the list. I'll read the words in random order. You point to the word after I read it. Then, you read the words in any order and point to each word you read.

Spell by sound substitution

Prepare a fill-in-the-blank word exercise. Then, dictate words to the student. Ask the student to repeat each word and fill in the first letter or letters of the word.

Teacher:	I'm going to dictate words to you. You write in the letters to make the word.

Spell whole words

On another sheet of paper, ask the student to say each word you dictate. Then, have her write the words. Use some of the same words and some new ones.

Spell words in sentences

Give the student a fill-in-the-blank sentence exercise that you've prepared in advance. If you are teaching a group, ask students to work in pairs to decide the correct word for each sentence.

Teacher: For each blank, put in a word that has the *-ill* word pattern. Any word that makes sense and follows the pattern is acceptable.

My daughter stayed home today
because she was _____.

When the winter wind blows, I
get a _____.

When I save enough money, I _____
buy a new car.

I have to pay my phone _____
by tomorrow.

Teacher: Now, you write a few simple sentences that use *-ill* words. Then, go back to the piece of writing where your spelling errors occurred and proof your piece for *-ill* spelling errors.

Teach complementary word patterns

If you are going to introduce more than one pattern in a single lesson, the patterns should be complementary. That is, you might introduce *-iss* and *-iff* or *-ell* and *-all* with *-ill* but not *-ark* or *-ent*. Patterns that are dissimilar visually or in their sounds are hard to remember if introduced together.

Teaching Syllabication

Being able to break words into syllables helps students figure out multisyllabic words they read. Students are ready to learn syllabication when they can distinguish consonants from vowels and recognize common blends (*br, st, bl*) and the digraphs (*sh, ch, th, wh*). This activity introduces syllabication.

Purpose: To teach syllabication as a strategy for word recognition and as an aid in sounding out longer words encountered in reading.

Materials: Flip chart or chalkboard.

Process:

> Understand what a syllable is

> Break words into syllables

> Use syllables as a guide to pronunciation

> Relate vowel sounds to syllables

> Compare syllable patterns

Understand what a syllable is

Ask students what they already know about syllables. Then, define and illustrate what a syllable is using several words of varying length.

Teacher: A syllable is a beat within a word. Each syllable contains one vowel sound. Here are words that differ in the number of syllables they have. As I say each word, I'll clap once for each syllable.

fan (1)	temper (2)
napkin (2)	cavity (3)
stop (1)	respond (2)
vacation (3)	safe (1)

Teacher: Here is another list. I'll read each word. This time you say how many syllables you hear in each word.

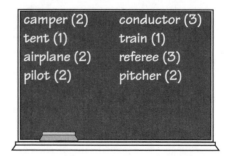

camper (2)	conductor (3)
tent (1)	train (1)
airplane (2)	referee (3)
pilot (2)	pitcher (2)

Break words into syllables

Teacher: I will teach you a way to break words into syllables. Using this tool you will be able to read longer words more easily. We'll start with a list of words. For each word, identify the vowels and underline them. Then, count the number of consonants between the marked vowels.

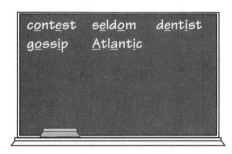

Teacher: How many consonants are between the marked vowels?

Student: Two.

Teacher: When there are two consonants between single vowels in a word, you generally split the word between the two consonants. One consonant goes with the first syllable and the other goes with the next. Now, split each word into syllables and I'll draw a line between the two consonants.

Use syllables as a guide to pronunciation

Teacher: When a single vowel is followed by one or more consonants in a syllable, the vowel is usually short (pointing to the same word list). Is each vowel followed by a consonant?

Student: Yes, so they are short vowel sounds.

Teacher: Now, read the words, emphasizing the short vowel pronunciations.

Relate vowel sounds to syllables

Show students that every syllable has one, and only one, vowel sound.

Teacher: (Using the same word list.) How many syllables does each word have? (Writing the students' answers next to each word.) How many vowel sounds are in each word?

Student: There are the same number of vowel sounds as syllables.

Teacher: Right. That's why the number of syllables in a word will equal the vowel sounds in the word. Underlining the vowels you hear is an important step in sounding out longer words. But remember that in some words not every vowel letter has a separate sound. Look at *airplane*. How many vowel letters does it have?

Student: Four.

Teacher: How many vowel sounds do you hear?

Student: Two—long *a* twice.

Teacher: Right. The same number of syllables that it has. You've learned some things about syllables that can help you when you come to long words in your reading and when you try to pronounce words that are new to you.

Compare syllable patterns

Teacher: All the words that we marked had the same pattern, VC/CV. There were two consonants between the vowel sounds, and the split came between the consonants. Now I'll show you another type of syllable pattern. Here is another list of words. First underline all the vowels. Then, count the number of consonants between the marked vowels. How many consonants are between the vowels?

Student: Three.

Teacher: When there are more than two consonants between single vowels you must look for common blends. Keep the blends together when dividing words. Common blends will stay together in the same syllable. To mark a blend, draw a single curved line under the blend.

Teacher: There are several rules about syllables. To help you practice identifying syllables in words with these two patterns, I'll give you words that have both types of patterns mixed together. In pairs, work on separating the words into two lists, one for each pattern. When you are done, I'll write what you say on the board.

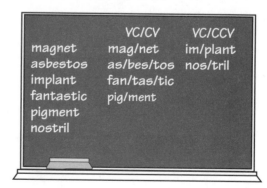

Developing Sight Words

The more words a reader recognizes by sight, the more efficient and fluent the reader becomes. The most effective way to develop a large sight word vocabulary is by reading as much as possible. Direct instruction of sight words, however, can help students learn particularly troublesome words.

You can use common sight words often. Use phonetically irregular words, such as *your* or *was;* phonetically irregular words that must be learned individually, such as *enough* or *through;* words with a common pattern that the student has not yet learned, such as *complete* or *invention;* or words that a student needs for specific situations, such as work.

Specific sight word instruction should be limited to four or five new words each lesson. Learning sight words depends on frequent review and having opportunities to use the words in actual reading and writing.

Purpose: To help students expand their sight word vocabulary for use in reading and writing.

Materials: Index cards.

Process:

> Identify the words
>
> Make flash cards
>
> Practice with the cards
>
> Use the words in context
>
> Read and write for communication

Identify the words

During a reading activity, the student can point out four or five words he wants to learn. During discussion, the student can also identify personal situations for which he needs to improve his sight word vocabulary. The student can also do a language experience activity that produces a text for reading from which he can select sight words.

Student: I need to read and write instructions for my job. I work as an auto mechanic.

Teacher: OK. You know your job and you certainly know the lingo. Let's do a language experience activity to help you learn to read the words that you have in your oral vocabulary. What kinds of work orders do you need to read and write?

Student: Well, in the summer, people's engines overheat a lot.

Teacher: Tell me what you do to troubleshoot when that happens, and I'll write down what you say.

The student dictates while the teacher writes.

Teacher: OK. I'll read this back to you, and you tell me if I've got it down right. Follow along as I read. Then, you read it. I'll help you with difficult words. You can reread several times until you can read it easily. Then, choose and underline four or five words or terms that you want to learn as sight words.

> Checking the Radiator
> 1. Check the water level. If it's low, look for leaks in the <u>radiator</u> or hoses.
> 2. Look for white or rust <u>streaks</u> coming from the radiator. If you see them, there's probably a leak.
> 3. Check the <u>coolant</u>. Make sure there's enough.
> 4. Check the front of the radiator for insects. Insects can prevent cool air from reaching the radiator water.
> 5. Check the <u>radiator pressure cap</u>. It needs to hold the correct amount of pressure. Otherwise the coolant can boil over and will cause overheating.

Make flash cards

Teacher: Write the words you underlined on individual flash cards. On the back, write simple sentences that help you remember the words.

radiator	The radiator is leaking.	coolant	It needs more coolant.
streak	Streaks are bad.	radiator pressure cap	Check the radiator pressure cap.

Practice with the cards

Flash each card several times, asking the learner to read it. If he has trouble, refer him to the place where the word can be found in the reading selection. Have the student review the word cards by himself.

Use the words in context

As the student practices with the flash cards, rewrite the reading selection in cloze format, leaving blanks for the sight words.

Teacher: Place your word cards in a horizontal row above these sentences for reference. Read each sentence and write your sight words in the appropriate blanks.

radiator	streak	coolant	radiator pressure cap

If the water level is low, check for leaks in the __radiator__ or hoses.

Look for white or rust __streaks__ coming from the __radiator__.

Check the __coolant__. Make sure there's enough __coolant__.

Make sure there's enough pressure under the __radiator pressure cap__.

Read and write for communication

If the sight words were taken from a reading selection in which the words recur, ask the student to continue reading. If they were taken from a language experience activity, you can suggest a new activity on the same topic. The student can also write new sentences containing the words, using the word cards for reference.

Teacher: This time, write a work order. You can dictate it to me or write it yourself, using the word cards for reference. We can practice more next session. Bring in any work forms you have for troubleshooting, and we'll practice with them.

Building Vocabulary

To become more familiar with words they have encountered in reading, students can learn how to play a word game called Clues and Questions.* Students choose words from their personal vocabulary lists, prepare clues or questions for each word, and quiz each other.

Purpose: To help students expand their knowledge of new vocabulary words.

Materials: Students' vocabulary lists, chalkboard or flip chart, and index cards.

Process:

Demonstrate how to make items
Help students prepare the cards
Play the game

Demonstrate how to make items

Ask several volunteers to select one word from their word lists and read the word aloud. Write the words on the board. Working with one word at a time, help students prepare a clue or a question that can be answered by the word. Clues can be a synonym or antonym, or a sentence with a blank for the word.

Teacher: For the word *tornado,* you might use any of these.

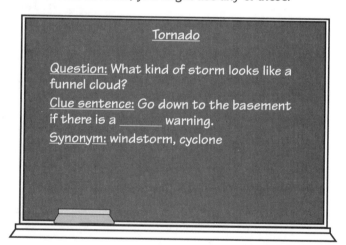

Tornado

Question: What kind of storm looks like a funnel cloud?

Clue sentence: Go down to the basement if there is a _____ warning.

Synonym: windstorm, cyclone

Help students prepare the cards

Teacher: Now, select two or three words from your word lists. Use one index card for each word. Write the word on the top of the card. Write your question or clue in the middle of the card. Put your initial in the upper right-hand corner of each card.

Play the game

Students form pairs or teams and take turns reading clues and guessing words, keeping score or not.

* From "Developing Content Area Reading Vocabulary," by T. W. Bean in the *Journal of Reading,* International Reading Association, 1978.

Teaching the Main Idea

In this activity students learn how to organize information into main ideas and details. Students need to know how to think about information as main ideas and details when they read and write. Students who are unfamiliar with the way texts are organized may find it very difficult to state the main idea of a reading passage or write a topic sentence before giving details. It is often easier for students to list details first and then use the details to decide on a main idea. To become familiar with this basic organizational pattern, students read, discuss, and write details and a main idea.

Purpose: To help students organize information into main ideas and details.

Materials: A brief passage in which the main idea and supporting details are clear, a flip chart or chalkboard, and index cards.

Process:

> Read a passage to remember it

> List each point from memory

> Say what the passage is mainly about

> Say how the other ideas relate to this idea

> Organize the main idea and details

> Practice writing the main idea and details

> Read a passage to remember it

Teacher: Today we're going to talk about an important way ideas are organized in reading and writing. Here is a passage for you to read. Read it and try to remember what it says.

> **You may want to learn
> to read and write,
> but going to school
> is not easy.**
> Maybe you don't have enough time
> for school and work
> and your family.
> Maybe your family and friends
> try to stop you.
> They don't always
> want you to go to school.
> Maybe you had a bad time
> in school before
> and you don't want to go back
> to the same thing.
> Maybe you don't want other people
> to know you can't read and write.

From "Going Back to School" in *Today's World: Family Issues*, by Linda Ribaudo and Darlyne Walker, New Readers Press, 1994.

List each point from memory

Teacher: Now, tell me everything you remember, and I'll write it on the board.

> you don't have time
> it's hard to go to school
> your family stops you
> you can't read or write
> you don't like school

Say what the passage is mainly about

Teacher: What do all these points tell you?
Student: It's not easy to go to school.
Teacher: Yes. They all relate to that idea, so that's the main idea. See, the main idea is clearly stated in the second half of the first sentence.

Say how the other ideas relate to this idea

Teacher: How do the points relate to the idea that it's not easy to go to school?
Student: They tell you why it's not easy.
Teacher: Yes. They all support the main idea.

Organize the main idea and details

To help students visualize the relationship between the main idea and details, you can draw a mind map. To show how the ideas are laid out in a text, write the main idea at the top of a list and show each point beneath it.

Teacher: All the ideas that fit or relate to a main idea are called details. We can make a mind map, showing the main idea in the center, and the details around it. When we read or write, the main idea often comes first and the supporting details follow it.

(you don't have time)   (your family stops you)   Going to school isn't easy

(Going to school isn't easy)   you don't have time
                                       your family stops you
(you can't read or write)   (you don't like school)   you can't read or write
                                                             you don't like school

Practice writing the main idea and details

Teacher: Let's practice this for ourselves. All of you have found ways to overcome the difficulties of going back to school. List the things you have done and I'll write the list on the board. Then we'll look at the list and write a main idea statement that includes all your ideas.

Teaching Comparison and Contrast

Making comparisons is a basic way to relate ideas. We all talk about how things are alike or different. Students need to understand how to organize information using the compare-and-contrast pattern when they read and write. In this lesson, students are introduced to the compare-and-contrast pattern for reading and writing.

Purpose: To help students organize information using comparison and contrast.

Materials: A reading selection that compares and contrasts two things, flip chart or chalkboard

Process:

> Introduce the compare-and-contrast pattern

> Make sentences

> Read, discuss, and write

Introduce the compare-and-contrast pattern

Teacher: One basic way we think is by comparing and contrasting. We look at two things and think about how they are the same and how they are different. We compare ways in which two things are alike. We contrast ways in which two things are different.

Make sentences

Teacher: Make up some sentences that tell one or two ways in which we are like one another and one or two ways in which we are different.

Students: Susan and Tanya like to go to movies and listen to music. Joe likes to play outdoor sports, but Jeff likes to watch sports on TV.

Read, discuss, and write

The teacher used a selection called "The Automobile Revolution" from a reading instruction series.

Teacher: Sometimes an author writes to show similarities and differences. That's what the author does in the selection called "The Automobile Revolution." The author talks about how cars changed from the way they were when they were first invented. Then the author tells how the changes in the car changed the way people lived. Let's read this selection together. We'll list some of the ways early cars were the same or different from the cars that came later.

The Automobile Revolution

In 1906, the automobile offered a picture of the snobbishness of wealth. When it ceased to be a symbol of wealth for the few and became a need for the many, great changes in American life occurred.

In 1906 the motorist had to crank the engine by hand—a difficult and dangerous business. Most cars were open. Going for a ride was like riding a motorcycle. Horses were a danger for the driver. Speed limits were low.

In 1916, only 2 percent of the cars made in the United States were closed; by 1926, 72 percent of them were. Automobile makers had learned to build closed cars that were not extremely expensive.

The number of Americans whose home and place of employment were at least twenty miles apart vastly increased. The automobile expanded Americans' sense of geography. The automobile revolution brought sudden death in collisions. It also gave birth to a new kind of personal pride.

From "The Automobile Revolution," in Book 6 of the *Challenger* Adult Reading Series, by Corea Murphy, 1988. Adapted excerpt from "The Automobile Revolution" from *The Big Change: America Transforms Itself 1900–1950* by Fredrick Lewis Allen. Copyright 1952 by Fredrick Lewis Allen. Reprinted by permission of HarperCollins Publishers, Inc.

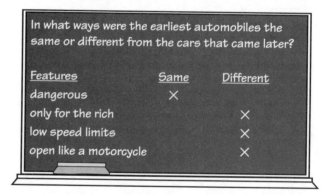

In what ways were the earliest automobiles the same or different from the cars that came later?

Features	Same	Different
dangerous	X	
only for the rich		X
low speed limits		X
open like a motorcycle		X

Teacher: Let's use the compare-and-contrast pattern to write a paragraph about computers. First we'll list some ways computers are the same as when they were first introduced and some ways they are different. Next we'll write a main idea statement to cover the information. Then we'll write sentences that say what computers were like when they first came out and how they are now. We'll end by saying how the changes in computers are changing the way we live.

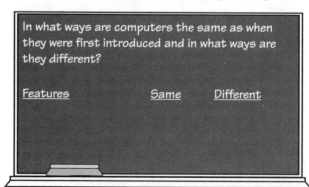

In what ways are computers the same as when they were first introduced and in what ways are they different?

Features	Same	Different

Teaching Cause and Effect

Thinking in terms of cause and effect is a basic way of relating ideas and is very important to everyday life. Being able to solve problems depends on locating the cause of the problem. Planning for the future involves thinking about cause and effect: "If I do this, then what will happen?" Stories often involve cause and effect, as one action causes other things to happen. This lesson introduces students to the cause-and-effect pattern for use in reading and writing.

Purpose: To help students understand how to organize information into cause-and-effect relationships.

Materials: Chalkboard or flip chart, a reading selection that presents information in terms of cause and effect.

Process:

Introduce the cause-and-effect pattern
Make sentences
Read, discuss, and write

Introduce the cause-and-effect pattern

Teacher: We know that some events cause others to happen. For example, water and soil make plants grow. We have different ways we can say how one thing causes another thing to happen. We can say, "The water and soil cause the plants to grow," or, "The plants grow as a result of having water and soil," or, "If you give a plant soil and water, then it will grow." However we say it, the idea is the same; we're expressing a cause-and-effect relationship. Do one thing (the cause), and another thing will happen (the effect).

Make sentences

Teacher: Did anything happen to you today, good or bad, that was caused by something else?

Students: I overslept because I watched TV late last night. The food I ate for lunch made me thirsty. I didn't do my homework, so I'm in trouble.

Read, discuss, and write

For this lesson, the teacher used an article called "The Great Hunger" from a reading instruction series.

Teacher: Authors often organize information to say what happened and what effect it had. That's what the author does in this reading selection. The author tells about life in Ireland in the middle of the 1800s, when the Irish people depended on potatoes for food. Let's read this together and find out what caused the "Great Hunger" and what happened as a result.

The Great Hunger

Life in Ireland in the 1800s was filled with hardship. Just about everybody in Ireland depended on the potato for food. Only a spade was needed to grow potatoes. The people did not need to buy a lot of costly tools. The people not only ate the potatoes themselves, but also fed them to the pigs, cows, and chickens.

Yet the potato was the most dangerous of crops. It did not keep and it couldn't be stored from one growing season to the next. There was no other food to fall back on if the potato crop failed. And that is exactly what happened in 1845.

In October, 1845, the blight hit the potatoes in Ireland. Six months after the disease struck, the people of Ireland were clearly starving to death. In the summer of 1846, the potato crop was poor again. Children suffered most. By April 1847, the children looked like old men and women.

Extremely frightened, people began to flee. By 1851, more than a million people had left Ireland. More than a million and a half others were dead. Thus in six years, Ireland was reduced from nearly nine million to six and a half million people.

From "The Great Hunger," in Book 4 of the *Challenger* Adult Reading Series, by Corea Murphy, 1985. Adapted excerpt from *The Great Hunger* by Cecil Woodham-Smith. Copyright © 1962 by Cecil Woodham-Smith. Reprinted by permission of HarperCollins Publishers, Inc.

After the class read the selection, they discussed what happened and completed a cause-and-effect chart.

What happened to life in Ireland in the middle of the 1800s?	
Cause	**Effect**
(What happened first)	(What happened as a result)
It was easy and cheap to grow potatoes.	People depended on potatoes for food. So did their animals.
Potatoes couldn't be stored.	Some people starved in the summer.
Blight killed the potatoes.	Many people starved. People were afraid and left Ireland. In six years (1846-1851), Ireland went from having 9 million people to 6 1/2 million people.

Teacher: Now let's use the cause-and-effect pattern to develop a paragraph. What problem would you like to write about?

Student: What about how good jobs are hard to get?

Teacher: OK. Let's use this chart to write about it. We'll list all the things that happen and what the effects are. Next, we'll write a main idea statement that says what we are writing about. Then we'll write sentences that tell what happens and the results.

Discussing Learning Styles

In this activity, students explore their own learning-style preferences and discuss how to benefit from learning-style differences during instruction.

Purpose: To provide the opportunity for students to understand what their preferred learning styles are so they can use them to their advantage.

Process:

Explore students' preferences

Discuss benefits of knowing about learning styles

Materials: A chalkboard or flip chart, a learning styles checklist.

Explore students' preferences

Ask students to complete a brief checklist on how they like to learn. (See the Learning Styles Checklist on page 178.) If students cannot read the checklist independently, read the information aloud. Together, make a class-profile chart, listing each person's name and ways they like to learn. Highlight the class's prevalent learning-style preferences.

Have students brainstorm personal learning preferences and write down each response.

> **Teacher:** Think about this question for a few minutes, and then share your answers: "When I have to learn something new, how do I like to do it?"

Ask students to cluster and label similar responses.

> **Teacher:** Now that we have everyone's responses, let's look at them and say which ones fit together. What is it that they have in common?

Speaking and Listening	Visualizing/Doing	Reading/Writing
talking about it	trying it	making a note
getting directions	using a blueprint	using a blueprint
asking questions	watching a video	reading about it

Discuss benefits of knowing about learning styles

People prefer to learn in different ways. Knowing how different people learn best can be helpful in planning cooperative learning teams. Different learning styles contribute to problem solving.

> **Teacher:** This information can help us plan ways to learn. Think about how you can call on your learning preferences in this class. How should we team up for cooperative learning and problem solving? Who would be good to partner with when you have an assignment that requires a learning style you do not prefer?

Learning Styles Checklist

Name _____ Date _____

Directions: Use this checklist to find the best ways for you to learn. Read each situation. Check (✓) one or two things that you would do in each situation. Do not check more than two responses for any situation.

At work, your boss tells you to do something. What do you do?
_____ 1. Read about how to do it.
_____ 2. Write down what to do.
_____ 3. Watch someone else do it.
_____ 4. Repeat the directions several times to myself.
_____ 5. Ask the boss to repeat the directions.

At home, you are about to begin a new project. What do you do?
_____ 1. Read the directions a couple of times.
_____ 2. Write notes to help me remember what to do.
_____ 3. Have someone show me how to do it.
_____ 4. Say the directions over and over.
_____ 5. Ask someone to read the directions to me while I work.

It's time to do the weekly grocery shopping. What do you do?
_____ 1. Look at the cupboards and think about what I need.
_____ 2. Make a list of everything I need.
_____ 3. Walk up and down the aisles and pick up anything I think I need.
_____ 4. Tell myself over and over again what I need.
_____ 5. Ask someone to remind me of what I need.

You are trying to remember something you learned in class.
_____ 1. Read it over more than once.
_____ 2. Write down the thing I want to remember.
_____ 3. Picture it in my mind.
_____ 4. Talk about it with someone from class.
_____ 5. Ask the teacher to tell me about it again.

Scoring: Add up how many checks you made for each number.
Number 1 _____ Number 2 _____ Number 3 _____ Number 4 _____ Number 5 _____

If you checked mostly numbers 1 and 2, you probably learn well by reading and writing. If you checked mostly number 3, you probably learn well by visualizing and doing things. If you checked mostly numbers 4 and 5, you probably learn well by speaking and listening.

Discussing Study Skills

This lesson helps students explore ways to increase the effectiveness of learning to read and write by approaching learning in an organized way.

Purpose: To help students consider what they currently do and what else they can do to improve their effectiveness in learning.

Process:

> Do self-assessments and set goals

> Schedule follow-up discussion

Materials: A study skills checklist.

Do self-assessments and set goals

Introduce students to the idea that good study skills provide ways to approach learning in an organized way. Developing good study skills involves experimentation, and requires much practice over time.

Give students a study skills checklist (see the Study Skills Checklist on page 180). Explore the various aspects of studying: studying on one's own, studying in class, reading and writing to learn, and locating and organizing information. Ask students to check one or two items in each area that they want to focus on.

When students have finished, go through the checklist section by section. Students who have checked specific items can make suggestions about how they might improve these skills and by when. Then, give students time to write in their ideas for improvement and their target dates.

Schedule follow-up discussion

During a follow-up discussion, students can share their efforts at improvement, describe what they do that is effective, and share difficulties that interfere with good studying. They can also share their experiences and strategies, and discuss their goals and achievements.

Note: Beginning students can establish good study habits by learning to write lists of assignments, keeping word lists in alphabetical order, and doing homework. Developing students can learn to take notes in class and find information in dictionaries and encyclopedias. GED students need a full range of study habits, from regulating their time doing assignments to organizing ideas for writing and keeping information in order.

Study Skills Checklist

Name _____ Date _____

Directions: Check (✓) what you already do and put a plus sign (**+**) next to what you want to work on.

Studying on My Own

_____ Study in a special place.

_____ Turn off radio and TV.

_____ Set a limit to study time and work to that limit.

_____ Make a things-to-do list and check off items as I complete them.

_____ Keep my books together and bring them to class.

_____ Other: _____

Studying in Class

_____ Be on time.

_____ Have homework ready.

_____ Pay attention.

_____ Try to ask good questions.

_____ Other: _____

Reading and Writing

_____ Look over a selection to get its general idea before beginning to read.

_____ Read the directions and think about them before beginning to work.

_____ Read quickly when I just need to find one piece of information.

_____ Slow down when I do not understand what I am reading.

_____ Make notes of things I have trouble with and report them to my teacher.

_____ Underline important ideas when I read.

_____ Other: _____

Locating Information

_____ Find words and definitions in a dictionary.

_____ Find names and numbers in the phone book.

_____ Use the table of contents to find things in books.

_____ Use the TV schedule to find shows to watch.

_____ Other: _____

Organizing Information

_____ Use alphabetical or number order to organize things.

_____ Make clusters of ideas so I can remember them.

_____ Use mind maps to organize ideas I want to remember.

_____ Other: _____

CHAPTER 11 THEMES: PUTTING IT ALL TOGETHER

A theme is a broad topic that engages and sustains students' interest and encompasses a variety of activities. The most successful themes are chosen by students and increase students' ownership of the work involved in instruction. When learners have identified a theme, a series of sessions and activities can be planned that focus on it, thereby providing continuity and relevance. Working on a theme strengthens the democratic process as students explore together and act on issues and ideas that affect their world.

The benefits of using themes fall into three areas: motivation, meaningful contexts, and democracy. When students have chosen a subject themselves, they are more motivated. If subject matter is of intrinsic interest to students, they cross over the barrier that separates school work from real life. Learning about subjects they are interested in can reduce students' anxiety about learning and allow them to stretch beyond their current level of work.

Organizing instruction around students' interests ensures a meaningful context for learning skills. When embedded in students' expressed needs, skills become useful, memorable, and more easily transferred to other situations.

Theme projects bring the process of democracy, with all its flaws and rewards, into instruction. In an active democracy, people identify shared problems and act together to solve them. People gather their own resources and knowledge, decide what more they need know, and then learn it. They work to solve the problem. Finally, they evaluate how well they did and decide what new problems must be identified. They reach out for help from other people. Theme-based instruction does the same. It builds on students' existing strengths as advocates for themselves and their families and as people who create change in their communities.

Much of what happens during a theme project is student-generated, thereby increasing students' responsibility for their own learning. As teachers, our role is to keep an eye on the larger picture and guide students toward the goals they have decided on. When students are grappling with a social issue, we can help them define the issue, put it in historical context, and recognize their own prejudices. If students need specific skills to complete a project successfully, we can introduce them at the appropriate time.

This chapter explains how to organize learning around themes, and describes how three actual theme projects were conducted on the topics of homelessness, dealing with bosses on the job, and HIV/AIDS.

Organizing a Theme

Theme projects are flexible ways to organize learning. They can be developed for any program and for students of all reading levels. Some teachers organize all instruction around themes, while others use parts of several sessions to address a theme. This section explains the process of organizing instruction around a theme. (See the Guide to Organizing Theme Instruction on page 191.)

Process:

> Choose the theme

> Find out what students already know

> Find out what other people think

> Decide what to do with what you've learned

> Evaluate and plan the next step

Choose the theme

There is no one topic or list of topics that will work with every group. A good theme is highly relevant to students. It is specific enough not to be overwhelming, and broad enough to be challenging and to take a significant amount of time to cover. Some themes that have interested adult learners are: being a nonreader, child care, domestic violence, relations between men and women, effects of drugs and gangs on neighborhoods, homelessness, dealing with work, and AIDS. The essential criterion is that the theme should come from the students.

It is crucial that themes be genuinely student-generated, not subjects we think that students should study or subjects that just interest us. In general, a theme of genuine interest to the students may be unsettling, emotionally charged (either highly negative or highly positive), personal, and complex. The more specific a theme is, the more personal it will be. "Being a prison family" may be specific to a group of students, while "the justice system" is too broad. "The education crisis" is too vague, but "how to help our kids in school" may be an issue of concern.

As students become experienced readers and writers, they may become confident enough to deal with more academic or unfamiliar themes. For example, GED students might choose to study the rain forest to help themselves prepare to pass the science section of the GED exam. Or they might research world religions as an approach to the social studies section.

Some groups can decide quickly on a theme. Others may need more formal opportunities to choose a theme by brainstorming possibilities and choosing a favorite. You may discover candidates for themes from hints students give in social conversation, activities they are involved in, and topics that make them lively and talkative.

Find out what students already know

There are many ways to help students discover and share their knowledge and beliefs about a particular topic. Questions like these can help students articulate what they know:

> If you were going to explain this topic to a person who knew nothing about it, what would be important to say?
>
> What have you heard about the topic from other people?
>
> What things have you experienced yourself?
>
> Have you ever read anything about this topic? What was it?
>
> What opinions do most people have about this? Do you agree or disagree?

To explore ideas and initial responses to the theme, students can first talk about their own personal experiences with the theme, or they can agree or disagree with a controversial statement about the theme. Next, they can explore their ideas in writing, and then share and discuss what they wrote.

For new writers, you can use the language experience approach to help students record their ideas. Write down what students say, and return the written statements to the students to read and keep as a reference. Other students can use freewriting to explore their ideas and get them down on paper. Because freewriting is unedited, stream-of-consciousness writing, it can be a stress-free way to generate ideas. Volunteers can read sections of their language experience writing or freewriting to the group for discussion.

After articulating, writing, and discussing their ideas, students should be ready to record facts and ideas they have about the theme. This record of collective knowledge becomes a resource that the group will return to again and again.

Find out what other people think

This is the research phase of the theme project. After reviewing and discussing the record of what they know, the entire group can generate a list of questions they would like to have answered. Some of the questions may be intended to settle disagreements about the truth of some items listed as facts. For example, some students insist that they know you can get AIDS from touching. Other students disagree and say you cannot. Both of these opinions are recorded as questions to be answered by research.

Once the group has decided what they want to learn, they find ways to answer their questions. Some students can do independent research in the library. For new and developing readers, teachers can make audiotapes from library materials that students can listen to while reading the material. Students can invite experts to speak to the group. Videos, photos, and field trips may all provide information and opinions for the students to discuss.

Include literature (fiction, poems, and plays) so students can gain a new and deeper perspective on issues. Students can read and discuss articles, poems, stories, and plays on the theme.

Return frequently to the list of questions in order to discuss possible answers. If the group comes to agreement on some answers, record them. At the end of the research stage, you may want to explore what students now know about the theme. Students can again discuss and write down their ideas and opinions. They can make a new list of things they know. Students can evaluate how much they've learned by comparing the new list with the list of things they knew about the theme at the beginning of the project.

Decide what to do with what you've learned

Now the group decides on a useful project that will allow them to contribute to the solution of the problem they have identified. Projects may range from preparing a written document for others to read, to social actions that can significantly change the material conditions of students' lives.

Some action plans students have developed include: publishing a pamphlet on AIDS for other low-level readers; producing a short play for young people on gangs and drugs; helping one student get justice from a housing bureaucracy; and writing letters to the editor and holding public meetings to get better education for their children. Actions related to themes have led students to successfully create a child-care cooperative, start a housecleaning business, and extend city services into the community.

At this stage students make a real contribution toward a solution to the problem they have identified. As proactive adults, they can take what they have learned and use it to address the problem. They can participate in the world and make it more accommodating to their needs.

Evaluate and plan the next step

When the project has been completed, the students review what they have accomplished, what stood in their way, and what contributions they each made. They may identify specific skills they learned and those that need more practice. Often, new themes emerge just as students are finishing a project. Students may have run into a barrier that they would like to tackle. Maybe a tangent that had to be deferred can be the focus of a new theme.

Note: As students work on a theme, they may encounter tasks that require a specific skill. Do they need to read brochures or encyclopedias? Do they need to use alphabetical order to locate numbers in the phone book? The moment the need has been identified is the best time to teach a skill. Interrupt the session for a teachable moment or plan a mini-lesson. Then, return to the project.

Sample: Organizing a Theme

Homelessness

A class of 25 students in a community college GED program chose to do a theme project on homelessness. Students worked on the theme for 21 sessions during a five-week period. They worked on the theme for half of each session. Homelessness would normally be too broad a topic to use as a theme, but it was successful for these students because of their various and differing personal connections to the topic.

Choose the theme (one session)

Teacher: What themes are you interested in exploring?

Students brainstormed a list of topics, discussed the list, and voted for their favorite. Homelessness won. All the students were at least mildly angry about the issue. Several students were living in transitional housing, and one had been homeless before he stopped drinking. In addition, the students had to pass through a gauntlet of desperate panhandlers and their dogs to get to class.

Find out what students already know (one session)

Teacher: What do you know about homelessness already? What do you think? To explore your ideas and opinions about homelessness, here are some questions to respond to in freewriting: Have you or anyone you know ever been homeless? How many paychecks are you away from being homeless? What would you do if you lost your home?

As students read their writing out loud, everyone in the class became aware of how close they all were to homelessness themselves. A few students believed that homelessness only happens to people who are lazy or mentally ill. There was an angry discussion on this point. Some students gained a new appreciation for family support that they had been taking for granted.

Students started journals on their study of homelessness. Their first entries were lists of what they thought they knew so far about the issue. The teacher wrote comments and questions in the journals every three weeks.

Find out what other people think (ten sessions)

Teacher: What do other people know? Where can we go to find out what others think?

In small groups, students generated questions and wrote them on pages of flip chart paper. Then the whole class categorized the questions. Some questions were:

What caused such a rise in homelessness in the last few years?

Are a lot of homeless people also mentally ill?

Do homeless people ever have jobs?

The teacher returned to the issue of the homeless being lazy. She helped students identify additional questions about personal versus social responsibility for homelessness.

Each small group chose a category of questions to research. They brainstormed ways to get information. When the small groups reported back, they borrowed each others' ideas and added to their own lists of resources.

The class did library research in their small groups, photocopying sections from books and magazines. They learned how to access back issues of newspapers and use microfilm machines. They used National Issues Forum materials, read poems about home and landlords, and read first-hand accounts by homeless people. One student organized a field trip to the homeless day center that he used to frequent when he was on the streets. The class also decided to invite in one of the panhandlers from outside the building.

Decide what to do with what you've learned (seven sessions)

Teacher: What can we do with what we've learned?

Students brainstormed a list of possible ideas:

Help the panhandlers get jobs.

Sponsor a panel presentation by homeless people for the whole school.

Find out more about what can be done and educate the public.

Raise money for shelters.

Open our homes to homeless people.

Join militant squatters who are trying to get city officials to open more shelters.

They chose to begin a dialogue about homelessness in the community college newspaper to raise awareness and increase volunteerism among the students.

To conduct the project, students did a wide range of activities. They contacted the newspaper and suggested doing a point-counterpoint pair of articles. They read and used the newspaper's guidelines for submission of articles, wrote individual articles, read and discussed them, and chose teams of people with different views to write the two final articles for submission to the paper.

They prepared follow-up letters to the editor, researched which agencies had volunteers, and created a volunteer resource list to publish in the paper.

Evaluate and plan the next step (two sessions)

Teacher: What did we learn and where do we go from here?

Students created portfolios of the work they had completed. They tested themselves on GED-style passages and questions related to homelessness that they had compiled during the theme. For the immediate future, they decided to focus on proofreading skills to prepare for the GED writing test.

Sample: Organizing a Theme
Dealing with a Boss at Work

In a one-to-one learning situation, a student and teacher explored the theme of dealing with a difficult boss. The student had often mentioned problems he had with his boss, so the teacher suggested that they pursue this as a topic for a theme project. They explored the theme in 24 sessions during a 10-week period, using a part of each session.

Choose the theme (one session)

Student: I'm having trouble with my boss. What do you advise me to do?

Teacher: I don't have much experience in employer-employee relations in your line of work. Let's explore the subject together.

Find out what students already know (four sessions)

The teacher and student had been exchanging journals for a while. They each kept a journal, read each other's journals, and responded to entries that piqued their interest. The teacher decided to use the journals to help the student explore his ideas about dealing with his boss.

Teacher: Why don't you start writing in your journal about what is happening at work? Write how you feel about it, too. I'll write in my journal about my problems with my bosses and how I deal with them. To record what you already know about the subject, write one journal entry describing everything you have thought about the situation. I'll do the same.

Then the student created a list of questions to research.

Teacher: If you could meet with someone who was an expert on dealing with bosses, what questions would you like to ask?

Student: What do you do with a boss who is no good? How do you say no to a boss and keep your job? What can unions do to help?

Find out what other people think (five sessions)

The student and teacher decided to interview experts. They knew of no one who was an expert on all of their questions, so they decided to talk to several people who could contribute ideas and information. They each listed three people to interview, and chose questions appropriate for each person.

Student: I could interview my union shop steward, another worker with a lot of experience, and my neighbor who is a retired supervisor and might see things from the boss's point of view.

Teacher: OK. I could interview the personnel officer where I work, an experienced co-worker, and a supervisor in another department.

During the interview, they asked each expert to recommend written material. Recommendations included the company policy manual, the union contract, a pamphlet on workers' rights and responsibilities, and the employee handbook. Many of these materials were too difficult for the student, so the teacher either read them aloud with the student, simplified and rewrote important parts, or read them to the student for him to retell. Using the language experience approach, she wrote down what he said, made a clean copy, and gave it to the student as reading material. To make sure that the adaptations did not alter meaning, the student showed the rewritings of the company materials to his shop steward.

The teacher found an appropriate short story and some poems on the subject. After checking with social service agencies, the teacher also found a short video on assertiveness that made a clear distinction between aggressive and assertive behavior. The student recognized that his boss was an aggressive type who didn't use good managerial skills. After that, the student was able to write about the boss in his journal entries in a more objective and thoughtful way.

Decide what to do with what you've learned (twelve sessions)

The student prepared a series of steps that he was willing to take at work to improve his situation. The teacher did the same. The student included plans to become more assertive and to use the company policies and union grievance procedures to defend himself when the boss overstepped his bounds.

The student and teacher carried out their own plans, step by step, reporting results to each other in journal entries that served as the basis for discussions. During this phase, theme activity was reduced to homework and brief discussions at each session. Both the teacher and student were able to improve their work situations.

Evaluate and plan the next step (two sessions)

The student and teacher reread their own journals and took notes on what they had each learned. The student included taking notes while listening, talking to people he didn't know well, learning facts about his union and his job, improvement in reading, and writing more often at home. The teacher and student both wrote that they learned problem-solving skills. They discovered that, when described in general terms, they had planned many of the same steps to solve their problems.

The issue of discrimination came up several times in the course of the theme. The student brought in a book he wanted to read on the subject, so they began to work on this new theme.

Sample: Organizing a Theme
HIV/AIDS

A small group of intermediate readers decided to study AIDS as a theme project. In the beginning, the focus was on how the students could stay safe from AIDS, but as time went on, the focus shifted to how to help young people stay safe from AIDS. The group used about half of each session to work on the theme until they reached the action stage. Then they used all the class time, plus some outside time, to finish the project. They worked on this theme for 21 sessions during a five-week period.

Choose the theme (one session)

During a break one day, the teacher heard the students discussing AIDS. Some students were worried that they or their partners might have been exposed. Some had strong religious beliefs against people with AIDS. When asked, all were enthusiastic about looking into the issue.

Find out what students already know (two sessions)

Teacher: Do you know anyone with AIDS? What should the United States do about the AIDS epidemic? Choose one of these questions and write for 15 minutes to get your ideas about AIDS on paper.

A very volatile discussion followed. To provide a calmer atmosphere, the teacher asked the students to write again. The second writings were photocopied for everyone to read silently or in pairs. The group then brainstormed their ideas. They set ground rules for discussing items on which they disagreed. They agreed to disagree if they couldn't reach consensus, and to respect others' rights to hold different opinions.

Find out what other people think (eight sessions)

Students listed questions such as these: Can you get AIDS from kissing? Do the tests really work? Can kids get AIDS? Then each student chose one question for the group to explore. The teacher helped the group include questions that raised disagreements: Should we lock up people with AIDS? Is getting AIDS a sign of God's anger at a person's lifestyle?

Materials used for research included health department pamphlets, a biography of Earvin "Magic" Johnson, newspaper articles, an article on the AIDS quilt, AIDS education comic books, National Issues Forum materials, and materials distributed by churches. Students got materials from social workers and friends. One student's child had received AIDS information in school that he copied for the group. Together, the students read a play about AIDS and poems published by an AIDS hospice program.

The group watched a video of a TV movie borrowed from an AIDS education program, and took a field trip to the hospice program. This convinced the at-risk students of the seriousness of the issue and increased empathy for AIDS sufferers.

Speakers invited by students included a person with AIDS, a public-health nurse, an AIDS education outreach worker, and a preacher. The students themselves contacted most of the speakers and arranged the visits. The visit from a man with AIDS greatly improved the tone of the discussions. Students shifted from arguing beliefs to exploring new information.

Decide what to do with what you've learned (seven sessions)

After discussing what might be done, students wrote lists of ideas to read to the group if they wished. Some of the ideas were: sponsoring an education forum on AIDS for the school, publishing an easy-to-read health pamphlet, creating a comic book aimed at the local community, and organizing a multimedia education event aimed at teenagers. Because they felt their children didn't have a way to get good information, the students chose to create a photo comic book for local teenagers.

Activities for this project involved developing a story line through discussion and role plays, creating a storyboard to show the main events in order, and talking to teenagers to check the appeal of the comic book and to get advice. Students used the school's camera, read the operating directions, staged and photographed the role play, and used the yellow pages to find a photo developer and printer. They conducted a small fund-raiser and wrote a proposal to the program director for funds to print the comic book.

Evaluate and plan the next step (three sessions)

As a group, students reviewed the work they had completed during the theme project and listed what they had learned. Items on the list included:

How you can get AIDS

How you can protect yourself

How to work a camera

How to use the yellow pages

How to approach reading material that is much too hard

As a test of what they learned, each student decided to write a letter to a young person they knew, explaining about AIDS. The letters were reviewed for accuracy by an outreach worker who had spoken to the class.

Based on the success of the comic book, students decided to create another one on another theme and began the process of choosing a new theme.

Guide to Organizing Theme Instruction

Teacher _____   Class _____

Directions: Ask yourself these questions as you develop theme instruction.

Choose the theme: What theme would students like to explore?
Where will we get ideas to choose from?
How do I make sure that the theme belongs to the students?

Find out what students already know: What do they know? What do they think?
What questions will stimulate discussion?
What question(s) will stimulate writing?
How will students discuss their ideas?
How will we record what students know?

Find out what other people think: What do other people know?
Where do we go to find out?
Do we have a list of student-generated questions?
What materials may help answer the questions?
Who might students interview?
What nonprint materials should we study?
What literature is related to the theme?
Which experts might students invite to speak?

Decide what to do with what was learned: What can we do with what we've learned?
What are ideas for projects?
What activities are involved?
What action plans do we want to make?

Evaluate and plan the next step: What did we learn, and where do we go from here?
What assessment activities should we do?
What was learned?
What needs more practice?
How can students continue to use what they learned?
What do we want to do next?
What theme do we want to explore now?